COMBAT AIRCRAFT

140 YOKOSUKA D4Y 'JUDY' UNITS

SERIES EDITOR TONY HOLMES

140

COMBAT AIRCRAFT

Mark Chambers with Tony Holmes

YOKOSUKA D4Y 'JUDY' UNITS

OSPREY
PUBLISHING

OSPREY PUBLISHING
Bloomsbury Publishing Plc
PO Box 883, Oxford, OX1 9PL, UK
29 Earlsfort Terrace, Dublin 2, Ireland
1385 Broadway, 5th Floor, New York, NY 10018, USA
E-mail: info@ospreypublishing.com
www.ospreypublishing.com

OSPREY is a trademark of Osprey Publishing Ltd

First published in Great Britain in 2021

A catalogue record for this book is available from the British Library.

ISBN: PB 9781472845047; eBook 9781472845016; ePDF 9781472845023; XML 9781472845030

21 22 23 24 25   10 9 8 7 6 5 4 3 2 1

Edited by Tony Holmes
Cover Artwork by Mark Postlethwaite
Aircraft Profiles by Jim Laurier
Index by Angela Hall
Originated by PDQ Digital Media Solutions, UK
Printed and bound in India by Replika Press Private Ltd

Osprey Publishing supports the Woodland Trust, the UK's leading woodland conservation charity.

To find out more about our authors and books visit **www.ospreypublishing.com**. Here you will find extracts, author interviews, details of forthcoming events and the option to sign up for our newsletter.

Front Cover
D4Y3 '601-46' of 601st Kokutai performs one of the final dive-bombing attacks of World War 2 in the last weeks of the conflict in the Pacific, its crew targeting US Navy warships of TFs 37 and 38 as they sailed off the coast of Japan's Home Islands. This aircraft is famous for the 'bomb piercing carrier' marking painted on its fuselage just forward of the Hinomaru. Originally formed as the air group for the carriers of 1st Koku Sentai, 601st Kokutai was reorganised as a land-based unit after suffering heavy attrition in the Mariana Islands and the Philippines in 1944. It was subsequently involved in the Okinawa campaign, with 601st's dive-bomber squadron becoming 1st Attack Hikotai on 20 February 1945 and providing personnel for Special Attack unit 2nd Mitate-tai. By war's end, 601st Kokutai had grown into a huge formation, with 100 aircraft on strength (*Cover Artwork by Mark Postlethwaite*)

PREVIOUS PAGES
Equipped with two 330-litre underwing drop tanks, a D4Y1-C of 151st Kokutai has its Atsuta 12 engine fettled between long-range reconnaissance missions at Rabaul's Lakunai airfield in 1943. The distinctive twin peaks of Tavurvur volcano can be seen behind the Suisei (*Tony Holmes Collection*)

CONTENTS

INTRODUCTION   **6**

CHAPTER ONE
DESIGN AND DEVELOPMENT   **8**

CHAPTER TWO
BATTLE OF MIDWAY   **16**

CHAPTER THREE
TRUK AND THE MARIANAS   **19**

CHAPTER FOUR
FORMOSA AND THE PHILIPPINES   **49**

CHAPTER FIVE
KAMIKAZES   **59**

CHAPTER SIX
D4Y2-S NIGHTFIGHTER   **89**

APPENDICES   **93**

COLOUR PLATES COMMENTARY   93
INDEX   96

INTRODUCTION

n 1938, the Kaigun Koku Gijutsusho (Japanese Naval Air Technical Arsenal) at Yokosuka commenced work on a dive-bomber in response to the Navy Experimental 13-Shi Carrier Borne Bomber specification issued by the Kaigun Koku Hombu (Naval Air Headquarters, equivalent to the US Navy's Bureau of Aeronautics) as a replacement for the Aichi D3A. When this requirement was released, the latter, which would play a key role in the early successes enjoyed by the Imperial Japanese Naval Air Force (IJNAF) in the Pacific War, had yet to be officially adopted for frontline service. The D4Y Suisei ('Comet') created by Kaigun Koku Gijutsusho would eventually become one of the finest dive-bombers fielded in World War 2.

Codenamed 'Judy' (from mid-1942, the Allies gave all Japanese bombers female reporting names, while all fighters were assigned male names), the aircraft endured an inauspicious combat debut during the Battle of Midway in June 1942. However, it eventually proved itself to be quite a dive-bombing and kamikaze asset during battles in the latter years of the Pacific War, sinking or heavily damaging a number of US Navy warships of great significance, most notably the aircraft carriers USS *Princeton* (CVL-23) and USS *Franklin* (CV-13).

While the D4Y possessed enviable handling characteristics when in a high-speed dive thanks to it being the most aerodynamic aircraft of its type during World War 2, like its predecessor, and many other Japanese

The Navy Experimental 13-Shi Carrier Borne Bomber was designed as a replacement for the Aichi D3A Navy Type 99 Carrier Borne Bomber, christened 'Val' by the Allies from mid-1942. The pilot of this example, carrying a single No. 25 (551-lb) Ordinary Bomb on its centreline, has opened the throttle, allowing the dive-bomber to gain speed as it accelerates along *Kaga*'s flightdeck at 0715 hrs on 7 December 1941. This aircraft participated in the second wave strike on Pearl Harbor later that morning (*Tony Holmes Collection*) military aircraft, the 'Judy' was hamstrung by design shortcomings. The most significant of these was inadequate armour protection for the crew and no self-sealing fuel tanks. This meant that when D4Ys – and most other IJNAF types – encountered US Navy fighters such as the F6F Hellcat and F4U Corsair, they suffered horrendous losses.

During the final months of World War 2, when it became apparent to the Japanese that there would be no victory for them in the Pacific, the IJNAF employed the 'Judy' in the dreaded kamikaze role. Although the D4Y excelled in this deadly task, the efforts of its crews proved futile against an enemy that was both numerically stronger and technically more advanced. Nevertheless, in one of the last combat actions of World War 2, a flight of 11 D4Ys commanded by Vice Admiral Matome Ugaki, who had been in charge of the kamikaze campaign in the defence of Okinawa, took off on a 'search mission' on 15 August 1945. Only three of the dive-bombers taking part in the final kamikaze operation of the war survived to return to their base at Oita, on Kyushu.

This volume details the history of the D4Y from its design and development through to its frontline use as a dive-bomber, fast reconnaissance aircraft, nightfighter and, finally, kamikaze weapon.

ACKNOWLEDGEMENTS

Numerous individuals deserve great thanks for providing crucial support during the writing of this book. First and foremost, thank you to my loving family, my wife Lesa, daughter Caitlyn and sons Patrick and Ryan, for tolerating my ceaseless words of enthusiasm and providing encouragement and support for this project. Thanks also go to David Pfeiffer (Civil Records Archivist), Nate Patch (Military Records Archivist) and the staff of the Textual Reference Branch of the US National Archives and Record Administration (NARA II) at College Park, Maryland. Thank you also to Holly Reed and the staff of the Still Pictures Branch of the NARA II. In addition, thanks to Archie DiFante and Tammy T Horton of the Air Force Historical Research Agency (AFHRA) at Maxwell AFB, Alabama, for providing additional research assistance and materials. Thank you also to Mark Eite (AFLO, The Mainichi Archives, Tokyo, Japan), Dr Yasuho Izawa and Yasuki Yoshino for providing rare, authentic Japanese-sourced aircraft photographs, and to Philip Jarrett and Joe Picarella for sourcing images from their respective archives.

The editor would like to express his profound thanks to Michael Wenger, editor of *The Emperor's Sea Eagle* (Arizona Memorial Museum Association), and Jim McCoy, Pacific History Parks' Director of Communications and Development, for allowing extensive text extracts to be used in this volume. Finally, a huge thank you to Osamu Tagaya for taking the time to provide new information for inclusion in this volume and to fact check the edited manuscript and proof the profile artwork.

CHAPTER ONE

DESIGN AND DEVELOPMENT

With the Aichi D3A1 Type 99 on the cusp of entering operational service, the IJNAF was already busy making plans for the design and development of the dive-bomber's replacement. To this end, in the spring of 1938, it had acquired the Heinkel He 118 V4, and production rights for the monoplane dive-bomber, from Germany. The previous year, the aircraft had competed with and lost out to the Junkers Ju 87 Stuka in the competition to find the Luftwaffe's primary dive-bomber. Powered by a 1175 hp Daimler-Benz DB 601A liquid-cooled 12-cylinder inverted-Vee inline engine, the V4 had arrived in Japan in the summer of 1938 following shipment aboard the *Kagu Maru*.

Designated the DXHe1 by the IJNAF, the aircraft underwent flight testing at Yokosuka. It attained a top speed of 260 mph (some 20 mph faster than the D3A1) during the course of the evaluation, greatly impressing IJNAF officials. In a subsequent flight, however, the DXHe1 suffered a catastrophic failure that caused it to disintegrate in mid-air, putting an end to plans to produce a modified version of the Heinkel for carrier-borne service.

Despite the DXHe1's premature demise in Japan, the test results obtained by the IJNAF during the aircraft's flight trials had a strong influence on the Naval Staff in respect to the requirements listed for the prospective replacement for the D3A1. Designated the Navy Experimental 13-Shi Carrier Bomber, the aircraft had to have a maximum speed of

Although built as a D4Y1, this aircraft later served as the ninth prototype of the D4Y2 series following re-engining with an Atsuta Model 32. It is seen here awaiting flight-testing at the Naval Air Technical Arsenal at Yokosuka in the spring of 1944 (*Philip Jarrett Collection*)

In the spring of 1938, the IJNAF had acquired the Heinkel He 118 V4, and production rights for the monoplane dive-bomber, from Germany as it sought to develop a replacement for the D3A. The previous year, the He 118 had lost out to the Junkers Ju 87 Stuka in the competition to find the Luftwaffe's primary dive-bomber. Once in Japan, it was designated the DXHe1 by the IJNAF and flight-tested at Yokosuka (*Tony Holmes Collection*)

288 knots, a cruising speed of 230 knots, a range of 800 nautical miles with a 250 kg bomb and 1200 nautical miles without a bombload, and the ability to operate from both large and small carriers.

The IJNAF wanted the new aircraft to possess a sufficiently high top speed to allow it to outpace enemy fleet fighters tasked with protecting carriers from attack. Its cruising speed also needed to be quite fast so that the dive-bomber could cover great distances more rapidly than the D3A1. Finally, as with all IJNAF aircraft, the dive-bomber had to possess a large radius of action so that it could target enemy carriers from beyond the range of their own fighter and attack types.

The team assembled by the Kaigun Koku Gijutsusho at Yokosuka to create an aircraft that fulfilled these challenging requirements was led by Chief Engineer Masao Yamana. He and his men designed a clean, mid-wing, all-metal aircraft that was on the small side for a two-seat dive-bomber. Indeed, although the aircraft's wingspan (37 ft 8¾ in) was less than that of the A6M2 Zero-sen single-seat fighter (39 ft 4 in), its fuel capacity almost matched that of the D3A1 in order to give the dive-bomber the range required by the 13-Shi specification.

To achieve this, the Kaigun Koku Gijutsusho installed internal fuel tanks that were larger than those found in the He 118. The tanks initially fitted in either wing were removed and converted into a semi-integral system due to problems with the limited space between the wings. The latter, having an area of just 254 sq ft, were, nevertheless, capable of carrying 1070 litres of fuel – just nine litres less than the fuel tanks in the appreciably larger D3A1/2 wings, which had an area of 376 sq ft.

Unlike the Heinkel, which had served as the inspiration behind Yamana's design, the 13-Shi featured an internal bomb-bay capable of carrying a 500 kg bomb. This allowed the machine to be considerably more aerodynamic than the Heinkel – it was also appreciably lighter and smaller. The aircraft's wingspan was short enough to obviate the need for a weighty wing-folding mechanism for carrier use. On the underside of each wing were three electrically operated dive brakes, installed directly ahead of each landing flap. The dive brake spoilers were an ingenious innovation that duly became a standard feature on Japanese military aircraft. When the flap was not in use, it served as a component of the entire airfoil, thus inhibiting inherent drag. When the flap was in use, the spoilers became a component of the fixed wing's trailing edge, creating a large gap between the flap's leading edge. This enhanced the flap's high-lift qualities.

Small ailerons, possessing lengths of only 40 per cent of the entirety of the wingspan, were fashioned for the 13-Shi prototype. These lightweight ailerons were truly unique in that the more usual Frise type moveable surface had been omitted and the balance tabs attached to the plane form, which was not as thick as an ordinary airfoil curve. This innovation was also applied to future Japanese military aircraft.

Due to the IJNAF's requirements for a sub-100 m take-off run when operating from a carrier flightdeck, and a reduction in the wing area due to the short span, the wings were designed with an aspect ratio of 5.6, with the taper ratio being 0.5°. The wings also possessed a slight sweepback angle, while their profile resembled that of a laminar flow wing. They were also tip stall resistant – a feature lacking in the wings of the D3A1. Moreover, the 13-Shi's wings exhibited little drag in flight and possessed superb stall characteristics despite the high wing loading associated with their short span.

It is interesting to note that the engineering methodology seen in the creation of the 13-Shi was subsequently adopted in the designs of future IJNAF aircraft.

The IJNAF instructed Kaigun Koku Gijutsusho to fit the aircraft with a licence-built version of the DB 601A known as the Aichi Atsuta. However,

This D4Y1, which force-landed (note the bent propeller blades) after returning to an unidentified airfield in the Central Pacific with battle damage, was captured in an unrepaired state by US troops. The engine covers have been removed to reveal its Atsuta 12 engine. The Aichi-built equivalent of the Daimler-Benz DB 601A liquid-cooled engine, the Atsuta suffered from poor reliability in frontline service (*Picarella Collection*)

Of the 2038 Suisei built between the spring of 1942 and August 1945, less than 200 were reconnaissance D4Y1/2-Cs. Included in their number was this early-build D4Y1-C of Yokosuka Kokutai, photographed in 1943 soon after its delivery to the air group from the Aichi Kokuki K.K. Eitoku plant in Nagoya. It has a flat windscreen, which was only present on the first 45 Suisei completed by Aichi (*PD-Japan-oldphoto*)

there were no completed examples available when the prototype D4Y1 was rolled out, so a 960 hp Daimler-Benz DB 600G (a handful of which had been imported by the IJNAF) had to be fitted instead. Thanks to the reduced frontal area of the liquid-cooled engine, the 13-Shi had a speed advantage of 15 to 20 knots over aircraft fitted with radial engines producing similar power. The Daimler-Benz inline engine utilised a cooling system that made use of high temperature and high-pressure water functions to maintain a steady hot water temperature and prevent vapour locks. The incorporation of an inline liquid-cooled engine into the design of the 13-Shi greatly enhanced the pilot's frontal and lower vision and improved the aircraft's handling characteristics in a dive and when landing on a carrier.

The prototype was rolled off the assembly line in November 1940 and successfully completed its maiden flight at Yokosuka the following month. The performance and flight qualities exhibited by the aircraft during the early stages of the flight test programme surpassed the IJNAF's aspirations, and the flight trials accelerated in 1941 with the delivery of four additional DB 600G-powered prototypes.

Although the development programme had enjoyed a promising start, a potentially catastrophic technical problem soon arose during simulated dive-bombing tests that threatened further progress. Fully armed with two fixed, forward-firing 7.7 mm Type 97 machine guns on top of the engine and a flexible 7.9 mm Type 1 machine gun for the radio operator/rear gunner, and carrying the aircraft's maximum bombload of 559 kg (one 500 kg bomb in the fuselage bomb-bay and two 30 kg bombs under the wings), the prototypes experienced wing flutter. This in turn caused cracks to appear in the wing spars. These issues came to a head when the fifth prototype broke up in mid-air, killing the test crew.

While the design team at Yokosuka strove to find a solution to this serious problem, planned massed production of the aircraft (officially designated the D4Y1 by the IJNAF) at the Nagoya plant of the Aichi

Tokei Denki K.K. had to be delayed. Pre-production examples that began to trickle off the Aichi line in the spring of 1942 differed from the prototypes in engine only, being powered by the 1200 hp Aichi AE1A Atsuta 12. The latter gave the aircraft an impressive top speed of more than 340 mph, making the D4Y1 more than 100 mph faster than the B5N2 then performing the reconnaissance role for carrier-based air groups. Although forbidden from dive-bombing until the designers at Yokosuka (aided by engineers from Aichi) had resolved the wing flutter problems, the D4Y1 could undertake reconnaissance missions once fitted with a K-8 camera in the aft fuselage.

Designated the D4Y1-C, the aircraft emerged from the Aichi plant at an almost glacial pace due to the IJNAF's limited requirement for dedicated carrier-borne reconnaissance aircraft. Indeed, only 25 D4Y1-Cs had been produced by March 1943. The addition of two 330-litre external drop tanks significantly enhanced the long-range capability of the aircraft, making the D4Y1-C a favourite among IJNAF reconnaissance aircraft crews.

In order to fulfil the demanding range requirements stipulated by the IJNAF when it tabled the 13-Shi specification, Kaigun Koku Gijutsusho had had to make the D4Y1 as light as possible. This meant that it lacked armour protection for the crew and did not possess self-sealing fuel tanks – a common trait seen in most Japanese aircraft of the period. As a result, D4Ys would suffer heavy losses during air combat in the major battles to come in the Pacific War.

By March 1943, the D4Y1's wing flutter problems had been corrected through the fitment of reinforced wing spars that made the flying surfaces more rigid. These had been added to the aircraft through a collaborative research effort undertaken by engineers from Aichi Tokei Denki K.K. and Kaigun Koku Gijutsusho. Finally accepted by the IJNAF as a dive-bomber, the D4Y1 went into full-scale production with Aichi as the Suisei Carrier Bomber Model 11 (it was given the reporting name 'Judy' by the Allies). The company had produced 589 D4Y1s (the majority of which were dive-bombers) by March 1944. A later production variant, which became known as the D4Y1 KAI Model 21, featured the addition of catapult fittings that made the aircraft suitable for operation from smaller carriers.

Two factory-fresh D4Y1s of 503rd Kokutai prepare to taxi out at the start of a training mission from Kisarazu in the autumn of 1943. The air group had been established at this airfield on 1 October 1943 with 36 Suisei dive-bombers and eight D4Y1-C reconnaissance aircraft. These were amongst the first D4Y1 dive-bombers to be completed with reinforced wing spars and improved air brakes. They also lack the distinctive Type 2 Mark 1 optical gun/bombsight protruding through the windscreen (*PD-Japan-oldphoto*)

Having had enough of the Atsuta's unreliability, and keen to maximise production by diversifying powerplant options, the IJNAF instructed Aichi to find a replacement engine. The powerplant chosen was the 1500 hp Mitsubishi MK8P Kinsei 62 – an air-cooled 14-cylinder radial of large diameter. During flight testing with this prototype aircraft from May 1944, the modified Suisei's performance was found to be virtually identical to the inline-engined D4Y2 (*Tony Holmes Collection*)

Despite Suisei units having suffered grievous losses in the handful of campaigns the aircraft had been committed to since its delayed service debut with the IJNAF, the next variant to enter production still lacked any crew or fuel tank protection. In fact, modifications to the D4Y1 were restricted to the installation of the 1400 hp Aichi AE1P Atsuta 32 engine. Production of the 'new' variant, designated the Model 12, commenced in May 1944 and ended at Aichi three months later, although its official adoption for service by the IJNAF did not occur until October of that year.

The near-identical D4Y2a Model 12A saw the replacement of the original 7.92 mm machine gun for the rear gunner with a 13 mm Type 2 flexibly mounted weapon. When fitted with catapult equipment, these aircraft were known as the D4Y2 KAI Model 22 and the D4Y2a KAI Model 22A, respectively.

The engine and machine gun changes were also incorporated in the Navy Type 2 Carrier Reconnaissance Aircraft Models 12 and 12A, or D4Y2-C and D4Y2-Ca.

By then, D4Y production was also being undertaken by the Dai-Juichi Kaigun Kokusho (11th Naval Air Arsenal) at Hiro, with 215 examples being delivered between April 1944 and July 1945. Some of the Model 12s built by the Arsenal were modified into D4Y2-S nightfighters through the removal of bomb racks, flexible rear-firing guns, carrier equipment and the fairing over of the bomb-bay, and installation of a single 20 mm Type 99 Model 2 cannon mounted obliquely at an angle of 30 degrees in the fuselage to fire upwards and forwards.

The poor reliability of the Aichi Atsuta forced the next major change for the D4Y. With the engine having proven to be labour intensive in operational service, the IJNAF instructed Aichi engineers to seek a replacement. They proposed fitting the aircraft with the 1500 hp Mitsubishi MK8P Kinsei 62 – an air-cooled 14-cylinder radial of large diameter. Its installation to the slender Suisei airframe of narrow cross

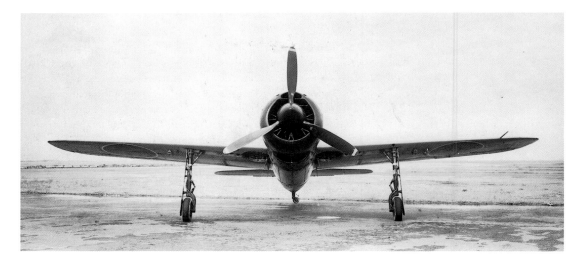

section presented numerous challenges. Consequently, a new, close-fitting, cowling that incorporated a supercharger air intake in its upper lip was designed. The cowling also featured smoothly tapered sides, which created only a minimal increase in drag.

During flight testing from May 1944 with a modified Suisei designated the D4Y3, it was found that the performance of the re-engined aircraft was virtually identical to the inline-engined 'Judy'. The only areas adversely impacted by the fitment of the radial were pilot visibility during carrier landings and reduced manoeuvrability on take-off. Designated the Model 33 (D4Y3) or Model 33A (D4Y3a – this variant featured a flexibly mounted 13 mm Type 2 machine gun for the rear gunner), radial-engined Suisei started leaving the assembly line in May 1944. By September, all D4Y1/2 production had ceased following the delivery of 986 examples to the IJNAF. The replacement D4Y3 would continue to be built through to February 1945, by which point 536 airframes had been completed.

Model 33 production reached its apex in December 1944 when 106 D4Y3s rolled off the line at Aichi's Eitoku plant in Nagoya.

Towards the end of D4Y3 production, Aichi modified aircraft to allow them to utilise three solid propellant RATOG (rocket-assisted take-off gear) units strapped under the rear fuselage. The rockets allowed fully armed Suisei to take off from small carriers.

No dedicated reconnaissance version of the D4Y3 was built due to the service introduction of the Nakajima C6N1 'Myrt' in the spring of 1944, the Navy Carrier Reconnaissance Plane Saiun ('Painted

Fitting a large-diameter radial engine to the narrow cross section airframe of the Suisei prompted Aichi engineers to design a close-fitting cowling that incorporated a supercharger air intake in its upper lip. The cowling also featured smoothly tapered sides that generated only a minimal increase in drag (*Tony Holmes Collection*)

The instrument panel of a captured D4Y4 after it had been fitted with American dials and gauge placards prior to being test flown from Clark Field in the final months of World War 2 (*Picarella Collection*)

Cloud') Model 11 being both faster and possessing a longer range than the D4Y2-C.

The final example of the Suisei to enter quantity production was the Special Attack Bomber Model 43 – designated D4Y4 by the IJNAF. Essentially a D4Y3 optimised for kamikaze missions, the D4Y4 was a single-seat variant that had the rear gunner's canopy faired over. The aircraft was also RATOG-capable, the rockets being used either to allow the Suisei to take off from a small airstrip or to boost its speed when in the final stages of a suicide dive on a ship. Capable of carrying a single 800 kg bomb semi-recessed in the now-doorless bomb-bay, the D4Y4 had a production run of 296 airframes between February and August 1945.

The last Suisei variant on the drawing board was the D4Y5, which would have been powered by an 1825 hp Nakajima NK9C Homare 12 air-cooled, 18-cylinder two-row radial engine. Featuring armour protection for the crew and self-sealing fuel tanks (both firsts for the Suisei), the D4Y5 was slated for production as the Carrier Bomber Model 54 from late 1945. However, the Pacific War ended before a single example could be built.

Just 2038 D4Ys had been constructed between the spring of 1942 and August 1945. During a similar timeframe, 7140 examples of the US Navy's Curtiss SB2C Helldiver – a contemporary of the Suisei – were completed and delivered to frontline units. The problems associated with the service entry of the D4Y1 (structural weakness and an unreliable engine) were principally a result of overambitious operational requirements stipulated by the IJNAF. The Kaigun Koku Gijutsusho (redesignated Dai-Ichi Kaigun Gijutsusho in February 1945) created an advanced design formulated in an 'academic bubble', with little practical regard for the limitations and realistic production capabilities of the Japanese aviation industry of the time.

Most aircraft of the later interwar period and World War 2, including those of the Japanese, took roughly three years, give or take, from design inception to squadron service. In the case of the D4Y, it took nearly five. In many ways, the development history of the Suisei, although it incorporated some extremely advanced design features, epitomised Japan's struggle to attain parity with the West in engineering and industrial capabilities.

This modified D4Y4 of Yokosuka Kokutai was captured at Yokosuka fitted with Type 4 RATOG. From early 1945, the IJNAF had outfitted rocket boosters to a small number of D4Y3/4s in order to enhance their effectiveness as Special Attack aircraft during the campaign in Okinawa and the defence of the Home Islands. It had been hoped the Type 4 RATOG would give an extra speed 'boost' in the final dive at the target, but the use of solid fuel rockets proved to be so fundamentally problematic that they were hardly ever used operationally (*NARA*)

CHAPTER TWO

BATTLE OF MIDWAY

Flushed with its success following the attack on Pearl Harbor on 7 December 1941, the IJN's Combined Fleet, under the leadership of Commander-in-Chief Admiral Isoroku Yamamoto, was cleared in the early spring of 1942 by the Naval General Staff to target strategically important Midway Atoll, in the Central Pacific Ocean. By seizing it in an operation codenamed *MI*, Yamamoto hoped to threaten Hawaii and, more importantly, draw the US Pacific Fleet's carrier force into a decisive battle that he was confident his air groups could win.

With preparations completed for Operation *MI*, Kido Butai (Mobile Force) commanded by Vice Admiral Chuichi Nagumo, which included all the fleet carriers for the operation, weighed anchor and sortied from Hashirajima anchorage in Japan's Inland Sea on 27 May 1942. As Nagumo's carriers got underway, the Pacific Fleet carriers USS *Enterprise* (CV-6) and USS *Hornet* (CV-8) entered Pearl Harbor, almost 1100 miles to the southeast. They were joined there the following day by USS *Yorktown* (CV-5), which had been badly damaged during the Battle of the Coral Sea some three weeks earlier.

With clear knowledge of Japanese intentions thanks to the efforts of US Navy codebreakers, a sense of crisis gripped the Pacific Fleet. In a Herculean, round-the-clock effort, minimum emergency repairs needed to make *Yorktown* seaworthy and battle-ready were completed in just three days. All three carriers had left Pearl Harbor, bound for Midway, by 30 May.

Heavily involved in the IJN's early actions of the Pacific War, *Soryu* had 18 A6M2s, 18 B5N2s, 16 D3As and two 13-Shi Carrier Bombers embarked in late May 1942 for the impending attack on Midway Island. The 13-Shi had in fact been modified into makeshift reconnaissance aircraft by the Kaigun Koku Gijutsusho, and one of them would be used in this role on the morning of 4 June when IJNAF aircraft were sent off in search of US Navy carriers (*Tony Holmes Collection*)

Non-aviator Vice Admiral Chuichi Nagumo commanded the IJN's Kido Butai during the Battle of Midway. He had overseen the attack on Pearl Harbor on 7 December 1941 and enjoyed further successes in the raid on Darwin and operations against the Royal Navy in the Indian Ocean during the early months of 1942. However, Nagumo's reputation suffered a heavy blow with the defeat at Midway (*Tony Holmes Collection*)

To attack Midway, Admiral Yamamoto had assembled an extremely powerful fleet that was divided into a Striking Force of Vice Admiral Nagumo's carriers of his Mobile Force, an Occupation Force and a Main Force of battleships under Yamamoto's direct command. The latter was to provide distant protection, and it did not take part in the battle. Indeed, Occupation Force and Main Force saw very little in the way of action during *MI*. The same could not be said for Nagumo's four carriers within the Striking Force, however.

The US carriers rendezvoused northeast of Midway during the afternoon of 2 June, advancing westward overnight to a position 260 miles north of the atoll.

A PBY from Midway spotted ships of the Japanese invasion convoy southwest of the atoll on the morning of 3 June, and a night torpedo attack by PBYs in the early hours of the 4th damaged the oiler *Akebono Maru*. On the Japanese side, Main Force intercepted a radio message in the predawn hours indicating possible enemy carrier activity north of Midway. Mindful of maintaining radio silence, however, Yamamoto's staff declined to relay this news to Nagumo, assuming that he, 300 miles closer to Midway, would have also monitored this signal. He had not. The IJN carriers closed on Midway from the northwest, blithely unaware that their American counterparts already lay in wait.

Nagumo's carriers (*Akagi*, *Kaga*, *Hiryu* and *Soryu*) had a combined total of 247 aircraft embarked, the vast majority of them being A6M2 Zero-sen fighters, D3A1 dive-bombers and B5N2 torpedo-bombers – the types that had wreaked havoc on Pearl Harbor six months earlier. On board *Soryu*, however, were two aircraft of a type that was about to make its combat debut. The second and third prototypes of the 13-Shi Carrier Bomber (the aircraft would not receive the official D4Y1-C Navy Type 2 Carrier Reconnaissance Plane Model 11 designation until July 1942) had been embarked in partial fulfilment of a request made by Nagumo's Mobile Force in October 1941, during the planning for the attack on Pearl Harbor.

The Kaigun Koku Gijutsusho had been instructed to modify two 13-Shi into reconnaissance aircraft for the operation, but these could not be made ready in time. After Pearl Harbor, the pace of operations precluded assigning these aircraft to Mobile Force until after the carriers had returned to Japan from their Indian Ocean raid in April 1942. Mobile Force had relied on B5N2 torpedo-bombers in the air search role up to then, and the IJNAF now wanted an aircraft with higher performance for a more effective long-range reconnaissance scout.

According to then-Lt Keizo Obuchi (interviewed by Naoki Kodachi post-war), who had been junior dive-bomber squadron officer aboard *Akagi* at Pearl Harbor, and who was now with *Soryu* at Midway, one of the 13-Shi suffered a mechanical mishap during a flight test after departing Hashirajima. A wing-mounted drop tank hung up on its rack and failed to jettison, thus preventing extension of the landing flaps when the time came to land back aboard *Soryu*. Therefore, the aeroplane was forced to come in 'hot', at high speed. It successfully hooked one of the arresting wires on the flightdeck, but its speed caused the wire to snap. This eyewitness testimony explains why only one of 13-Shi was operational at the time of the Midway battle.

The aircraft, marked with the tail code BI-201, was duly sent off on the morning of 4 June in search of the US Navy carriers. Its two-man crew effectively surveilled the vessels during the battle, marking a successful operational debut for the Suisei. However, upon returning to *Soryu*, the crew of the lone 13-Shi found their carrier ablaze – the result of successful attacks by US Navy SBD-3 Dauntless dive-bombers flying from the three US Navy carriers.

Hiryu, Kido Butai's sole surviving operational carrier by the afternoon of 4 June, manoeuvres hard to port whilst coming under attack from USAAF B-17 Flying Fortresses. The lone 13-Shi was forced to land on board *Hiryu* when, upon returning to *Soryu*, the crew found their carrier ablaze after it had been attacked by SBD-3 dive-bombers (*Tony Holmes Collection*)

By then, only *Hiryu* remained undamaged, and the 13-Shi made a successful landing on the carrier. Its senior officers were reportedly 'shocked' when they were informed by the aircraft's crew that three American carriers had been sent to counter Operation *MI*. The crew had indeed radioed its discovery of the enemy carriers, but the message was not received by *Hiryu*, and so time elapsed until the 13-Shi returned and the report was made in person. A number of sources have claimed that the aeroplane's radio transmitter was defective, but there appears to be documentation of some other vessels in the task force receiving the transmissions from the 13-Shi, suggesting that the fault lay with some quirk of atmospheric disturbance.

As a direct result of the lone aircraft's successful reconnaissance mission, two effective air strikes were launched from *Hiryu* that inflicted heavy damage on *Yorktown*. The carrier, hit by both bombs and torpedoes, was left dead in the water. It was ultimately finished off by torpedoes from the IJN submarine *I-168*. *Hiryu* was eventually attacked by US Navy carrier aircraft late in the afternoon of 4 June, and it sank the following morning after the crew was ordered to abandon ship and the vessel was scuttled. 13-Shi BI-201 was amongst the aircraft that went down with the carrier.

Although *Soryu*'s lone serviceable 13-Shi was the first Suisei to see operational service, the fourth prototype had actually been assigned to land-based 3rd Kokutai (Air Group), equipped with A6M2s and flying from recently captured Manado, in the Dutch East Indies, in January 1942. However, technical problems with this aircraft prevented it from taking part in operations, and it was sent back to Japan. After thorough maintenance and modifications to work out the problems, the prototype was embarked on board the carrier *Shokaku* in time for the Battle of Santa Cruz in October 1942.

CHAPTER THREE

TRUK AND THE MARIANAS

A D4Y1-C of 151st Kokutai undergoes routine maintenance at Rabaul's Lakunai airfield sometime after the air group was activated there on 15 April 1943. The aircraft's factory-applied Hinomaru was originally bordered by a white square, although this was painted over once the aircraft was posted overseas – hence the darker block of paint behind the roundel. 151st Kokutai markings were rather unique at this time, as its Suisei were bereft of unit codes on the tail. Instead, each D4Y1-C simply had an individual aircraft number (*PD-Japan-oldphoto*)

s noted in the previous chapter, the next action seen by the Suisei again involved a solitary example being used in the reconnaissance role, with the fourth prototype 13-Shi being flown from *Shokaku* during the Battle of Santa Cruz on 26 October 1942. Five months later, two D4Y1-Cs were assigned to 253rd Kokutai at Rabaul, on the island of New Britain in New Guinea, the land-based fighter unit being equipped with 48 A6M2s and maintaining detachments at Kavieng, Buka Island and Surumi.

253rd Kokutai's reconnaissance flight was absorbed into 151st Kokutai upon the latter's activation in the field at Rabaul on 15 April 1943. The unit was primarily equipped with the equally rare twin-engined Nakajima J1N1-C 'Irving' (known to the IJNAF as the Type 2 Land Reconnaissance aircraft).

Although only a small number of Suisei were ever on strength with 151st Kokutai, and these aircraft almost certainly suffered from the technical maladies that afflicted the D4Y1, the unit routinely flew long-range reconnaissance missions for Rabaul-based fighter and bomber units. Lone D4Y1-Cs provided aerial intelligence of the Admiralty Islands, Guadalcanal, Finschhafen and Brown Atoll (known as Eniwetok Atoll to the Allies) during the various actions fought in the Southwest Pacific in 1943–44. The majority of these flights emanated from Rabaul, although a number of missions were also flown from Truk Atoll, 785 miles due north of Rabaul.

Despite few details having emerged of specific operations flown by the Suisei of 151st Kokutai, which disbanded on 10 July 1944, it would appear that at least four D4Y1-Cs fell to US Navy fighters during long-ranging reconnaissance missions. The 'Judy' had never previously been seen by Allied pilots prior to entering service with 151st Kokutai, but the Imperial Japanese Army Air Force (IJAAF) Kawasaki Ki-61 'Tony' fighter was a familiar type. The 'Tony', like the 'Judy', was powered by an inline engine, so both aircraft looked similar in profile. Therefore, the single 'Tonys' claimed by VF-33 over Fauro Island, in the Shortland Islands archipelago, on 25 July, by VF-38 between Ballale and Shortland islands on 16 September, by VF-33 east of Kahili on 20 October, and by VF-40 south of Choiseul Island two days later were almost certainly lone D4Y1-Cs flying from Rabaul.

501st Kokutai would give the strengthened D4Y1 dive-bomber its operational debut in its originally intended design role flying from Rabaul in October 1943, the unit being equipped with 20 Suisei. The aircraft would also play a minor part in ill-fated Operation *Ro-Go* the following month.

Throughout that year, Anglo-American forces had steadily moved up the Solomon Islands chain, with their ultimate objective being the destruction of the Japanese air and naval stronghold at Rabaul. By achieving the latter, the Allies would break the enemy's hold on the Bismarck Archipelago off the northeastern coast of New Guinea. In the early autumn the Joint Chiefs of Staff approved Vice Admiral William Halsey's plan to establish airfields on the island of Bougainville that would bring Rabaul within range of Allied fighters and medium bombers. Halsey's planning staff duly decided to capture an isolated section of the west coast of Bougainville at Cape Torokina, in Empress Augusta Bay, and scheduled the invasion for 1 November 1943.

The US Navy's growing strength in the Central Pacific and Allied progress in the Solomons presented Japan's Imperial Headquarters with a dilemma. How and where to defend against the next Allied attack? In late September 1943 Imperial Headquarters issued its 'New Operational Policy', which called for a determined defence of all Japanese positions so as to gain time to rebuild before taking the offensive in 1944. Holding Rabaul was vital to this defensive policy. The IJN still hoped to defeat the US Pacific Fleet in a decisive battle, and had moved the Combined Fleet out of its anchorage at Truk following the 5 October raid on Wake Island in the hope of engaging Task Force (TF) 14. However, when no invasion of Wake followed, the Combined Fleet returned to its heavily defended anchorage at Truk – the IJN's largest base of operations in the South Pacific.

Instead, Admiral Mineichi Koga, Commander-in-Chief of the Combined Fleet, decided to strip his carriers of their entire air strength so as to reinforce 11th Koku Kantai (Air Fleet) on Rabaul as part of Operation *Ro-go* – the disastrous attack on US naval forces in the Solomons, which was undertaken in an attempt to halt Allied air strikes on Rabaul. At the end of October, aircraft from the air groups of 1st Koku Sentai (Carrier Division) – 82 Zero-sens, 45 'Vals', 40 'Kates' and six 'Judys' – from the carriers *Zuikaku*, *Shokaku* and *Zuiho* moved to Rabaul to join approximately 200 IJNAF aircraft already stationed

D4Y1-C '01-070' of 501st Kokutai was captured virtually intact by the 1st Marine Division at Hoskins airfield, on the north coast of New Britain, in early May 1944. This Suisei was almost certainly the aircraft recorded in 501st Kokutai's combat log as having crash-landed at this location on 28 January 1944. Its data plate was marked with Aichi's manufacturer construction number 3193, with the '3' digit being a dummy number. The Suisei's actual construction number was 193 *(Michael J Claringbould Collection)*

there. 1st Koku Sentai arrived in Rabaul on 1 November 1943 – the day American forces invaded Bougainville.

Rabaul had been targeted by the USAAF's Fifth Air Force in the weeks leading up to the landings at Bougainville, and the first major action involving the newly arrived fighters of 1st Koku Sentai saw them intercept just such a raid when New Guinea-based B-25 Mitchell medium bombers, and their P-38 Lightning escorts, attacked on 2 November. At least one D4Y1 of 501st Kokutai took part in this action armed with 30 kg and 60 kg air-to-air phosphorus bombs.

Between 5 and 13 November, the IJNAF suffered heavy losses in a series of attacks on the US fleet south of Bougainville and during the defence of Rabaul from American carrier-based aircraft. On the 5th, during the opening strike on Rabaul, US Navy squadrons had claimed 28 defending aircraft shot down. Amongst the latter were five identified as 'Tonys' (one of which was credited to TBM Avenger-equipped VT-12). With few IJAAF fighters based in this area, these aircraft were probably D4Y1s of 501st Kokutai.

There is solid photographic evidence, however, of Ki-61 'Tony' fighters at Rabaul, the imagery being taken by low-flying B-25s during raids in October 1943. At present, no detailed information has turned up from Japanese sources concerning these 'Tonys'. It is unclear whether they were an active detachment based at Rabaul or repaired fighters (the IJAAF operated a shipboard aircraft repair depot there) awaiting transfer to New Guinea, where the Ki-61 units were actually based. So some 'Tonys' were definitely at Rabaul at this time. While many reported Allied sightings of 'Tonys' in the area in the autumn of 1943 were undoubtedly misidentifications of 'Judys', one cannot say, categorically, that they all were.

It is possible that the problems US Navy pilots had in identifying the 'Judy' during this brief campaign were further compounded by the fact that 501st Kokutai used its small number of Suisei as makeshift fighters. Armed with air-to-air phosphorus bombs, 'Judys' were scrambled when Japanese long-range early warning radar detected an incoming raid by USAAF B-24 Liberator or B-25 Mitchell bombers or carrier-based US Navy attack aircraft.

The D4Y1 pilots would endeavour to position their aircraft over a formation of bombers and then drop their ordnance. The bombs were time-fused, and assuming the attacking Suisei was at the correct height above the bombers, they would explode in the middle of the formation.

In theory, the exploding ordnance would cause the formation to scatter, or even hit and set fire to a bomber. In practice, they had almost no effect. They rarely damaged Allied bombers, and the bombs' spectacular pyrotechnics even more rarely caused any reaction in a high-altitude formation. The main result of these efforts was to give Allied fighter pilots an opportunity to shoot down vulnerable D4Y1s that were no match for Hellcats and Corsairs, thinking they were inline-engined Ki-61s.

Following the Rabaul strike on 11 November, the IJNAF launched a counter-attack against TF 38. 1st Koku Sentai sortied 27 'Val' dive-bombers and 14 'Kate' torpedo-bombers, with an escort of 33 Zero-sen fighters. The formation was possibly accompanied by a handful of D4Y1 dive-bombers and D4Y1-C reconnaissance aircraft.

The Japanese attack came in four waves, but none of TF 38's carriers suffered any damage. In the confused combat in defence of the task force, the US Navy fighter pilots claimed 137 Japanese aeroplanes shot down – considerably more than had actually participated in the attack. Regardless of the precise number shot down, Japanese losses were heavy. Amongst the aircraft claimed to have been destroyed were six 'Tony' fighters. No such aircraft participated in this mission, so the claims by pilots from VF-9 and VF-17 were almost certainly for D4Y1s from 501st Kokutai during what was probably the aircraft's combat debut as a dive-bomber.

By the time 1st Koku Sentai returned to Truk on 13 November, just 52 of the 173 aircraft sent to New Britain two weeks earlier to defend Rabaul survived.

The remaining Suisei from 151st and 501st Kokutais (the latter unit was down to ten D4Y1s by 1 December) were sporadically encountered by US Navy fighters as they flew reconnaissance missions from Rabaul, with VF-17, VF-33 and VF-40 claiming four 'Tonys' shot down between them up to the end of February 1944.

501st Kokutai was also transferred to Truk in late January 1944 as Rabaul was all but abandoned by the IJNAF. Assigned to 22nd Koku Sentai and also equipped with 25 A6M3/5 fighters, the unit had barely had time to familiarise itself with its new base in the Caroline Islands when Truk was targeted by TF 58's Fast Carrier Task Force on 17–18 February in a raid codenamed Operation *Hailstone*. Although more than 120 IJNAF aircraft were claimed to have been shot down by US Navy fighters during the Truk strike, not one of them was identified as an inline-engined type – i.e. a 'Tony' or a 'Judy'.

Bronzed aircraft mechanics from 523rd Kokutai perform open-air maintenance on Tinian in the spring of 1944. The Atsuta 12 engine's designation label A1T1 C101 is clearly visible on the uncowled engine block. The air group had as many as 40 Suisei on the island, with the aircraft flying from both Ushi Point and Gurguan Point airfields (*Tony Holmes Collection*)

Lt Zenji Abe was in command of 36 dive-bombers (including nine D4Y1s) from 652nd Kokutai embarked in three carriers of the 2nd Koku Sentai during Operation *A-Go*. A veteran of early Pacific War carrier-based operations, including the attack on Pearl Harbor, Abe and his observer were one of the very few Suisei crews to survive the slaughter of the 'Great Marianas Turkey Shoot' (*Michael Wenger Collection*)

Combined Fleet in the late spring of 1944 when the IJN chose to take a stand in Operation *A-Go*. This clash, fought off the Mariana Islands chain in the Central Pacific on 19–20 June, would ultimately result in yet another defeat for the Japanese and signal the end of the IJNAF as an effective fighting force.

Lt Zenji Abe would participate in this action, leading his mixed force of dive-bombers from *Junyo*. He described the lead up to *A-Go* in *The Emperor's Sea Eagle*;

'With the situation in the Pacific growing more tense with each passing day, and with training in Iwakuni still incomplete, Combined Fleet issued an order, or "strategic plan", on 3 May;

'"Combined Fleet has determined its principal target area to be from south of the Central Pacific Ocean to north of New Guinea. The fleet will concentrate in decisive strength at this position, and, cooperating with other friendly forces, destroy at once the advancing enemy force, and especially, destroy enemy surface forces so as to completely smash the enemy's ability to attempt a counterattack."

'Consequently, 652nd Kokutai now moved to an advanced base in the south, delivering all of its crew and aircraft to 2nd Koku Sentai. I left Iwakuni airfield for Suonada in the Inland Sea near Yamaguchi, leading nine Suisei. With the wind at nearly ten metres per second, the sea below lay covered in whitecaps and spray. Finding the carrier force, I passed over *Junyo* at 200 m altitude. For nearly a year-and-a-half, I had been away from the sea and that particular ship. Then I spied the signal, "Relative wind speed 18 m; prepare to land on carriers".

'Alone, I left the formation, entered the landing course and extended my landing gear. As *Junyo* had never before landed the new Suisei aircraft type, I was aware that key officers, rigid with tension, were all watching my approach. But with no turbulence rocking the carrier, I shaped an ideal glide path, turned into the wake of the carrier, and lowered the tailhook. After catching the second wire, I came to rest at the best position on deck. "It's alright! Keep receiving the other aircraft", I advised the chief aeronautics officer.

'After reporting to the take-off/landing command post, I watched intently as the balance of my division landed. Unfortunately, one aircraft missed the centreline of the deck; in an instant it fell into the sea off the port bow. The plane guard destroyer following 800 m astern went to the rescue at flank speed, but the Suisei vanished beneath the surface of the choppy sea.

'Our carrier division took up its duty station off Tawi-Tawi, the southeast tip of the Philippines. On that day we traversed the Bungo Channel, passed into the Pacific Ocean and joined forces with the battleship *Musashi*, in company with *Chiyoda*, *Chitose* and *Zuiho* – the latter three were converted flattops of 3rd Koku Sentai [with aircraft of 653rd Kokutai embarked – there were no Suisei assigned to this air group, however].

'While the fleet steamed off the Philippine Islands over the next six days, the air groups of the six carriers rotated through their daily flight schedules, with each carrier sending aloft van and anti-submarine patrols. These patrols should have afforded an opportunity to season our crews and fine-tune their maintenance of the group's aircraft, but due to light winds then prevalent in our operating area, there was no chance for our dive-bombers to take part. Weather statistics recorded during June show that the wind velocity in the Central Pacific was less than three metres per second.

'It was indeed a grand fleet which had assembled in full force when we arrived at Tawi-Tawi on 16 May. The large aircraft carriers of 1st Koku Sentai – *Taiho*, *Shokaku* and *Zuikaku* – arrived two days after their air groups completed training at land bases near Singapore, while the carriers themselves lay in Lingga harbour, near the refineries at Palembang, in Sumatra, known for its oil and refining facilities.

'Named 1st Koku Sentai, and under the command of Vice Admiral Jisaburo Ozawa, our force was formidable – 57 ships, including nine aircraft carriers (with 439 aircraft embarked) and five battleships. However, the American Fifth Fleet that sortied from Majuro anchorage in the Marshall Islands under the command of Admiral Raymond Spruance was even larger. It had 112 ships, including 15 aircraft carriers (with 900 aircraft embarked) and seven battleships.

'We soon discovered that the Tawi-Tawi anchorage was practically held under guard by American submarines. By early June, four of our patrolling destroyers had succumbed to enemy torpedoes. In spite of such dangers and hardships, we felt compelled to enter the open sea to conduct our much needed flight training, as the overall skill level and state of training was low in most of the air groups, even by the standards of the time. Moreover, we found that our aircraft could not be maintained in tiptop shape unless they flew.

'Although *Junyo*'s group had opportunities to fly and conduct exercises four or five times while the fleet lay anchored, my uneasiness grew as I had not had a single chance to fly my Suisei owing to the light winds. Fortunately, the Suisei groups of 1st Koku Sentai – *Taiho*, *Shokaku* and *Zuikaku* [601st Kokutai had 70 D4Y1s split between the three carriers] – operated under no such restrictions owing to those ships' longer flightdecks [250 m] and their higher top speed of 35 knots. 1st Koku Sentai spent almost a month in the vicinity of Tawi-Tawi.

'One day a study meeting convened at the anchorage, with key officers from each warship taking part. According to a staff officer's explanation, the key objective of Operation *A-Go* was to carry out pre-emptive strikes against enemy task forces then operating in the Marianas by using "out-of-range" tactics. We hoped to keep a sufficient distance between our force and the American carriers so as to ensure that they could not attack us without risking the total sacrifice of their carrier air groups.

'With the Japanese carrier force thus assembled, our next step was to close on the enemy fleet and send the American ships to the bottom, cooperating with various land-based Naval Air Groups in the vicinity. It was thought at the time that our "out-of-range" tactics had a realistic chance of success. Notwithstanding certain numerical and technological advantages enjoyed by the Americans, Japanese carrier-based aircraft still

COLOUR PLATES

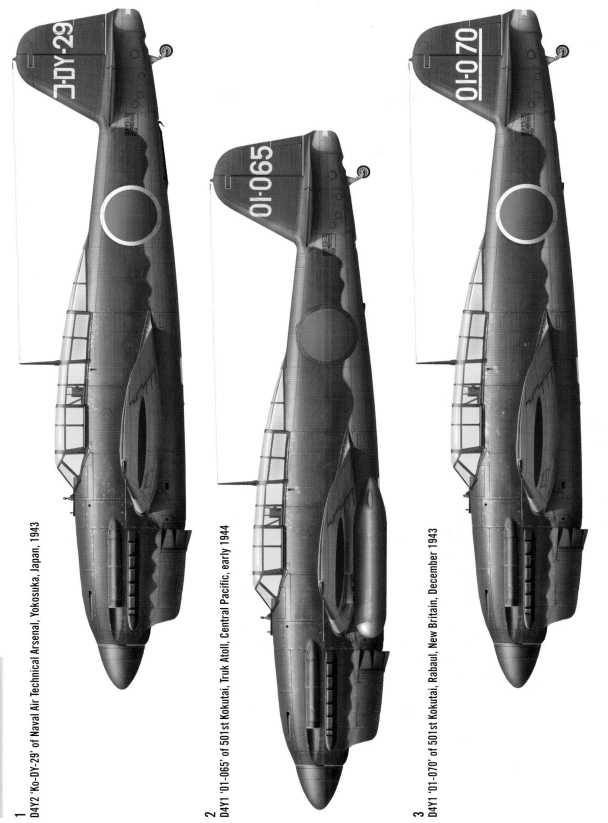

1
D4Y2 'Ko-DY-29' of Naval Air Technical Arsenal, Yokosuka, Japan, 1943

2
D4Y1 '01-065' of 501st Kokutai, Truk Atoll, Central Pacific, early 1944

3
D4Y1 '01-070' of 501st Kokutai, Rabaul, New Britain, December 1943

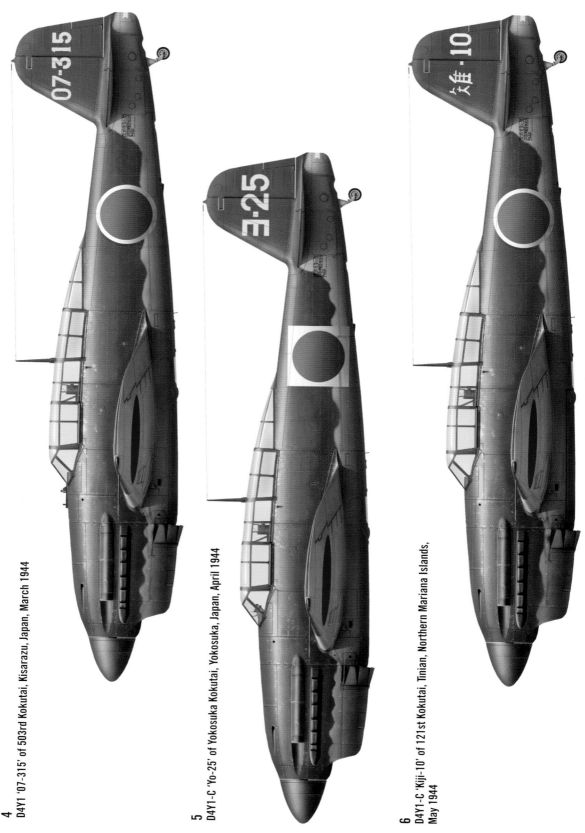

4
D4Y1 '07-315' of 503rd Kokutai, Kisarazu, Japan, March 1944

5
D4Y1-C 'Yo-25' of Yokosuka Kokutai, Yokosuka, Japan, April 1944

6
D4Y1-C 'Kiji-10' of 121st Kokutai, Tinian, Northern Mariana Islands,
May 1944

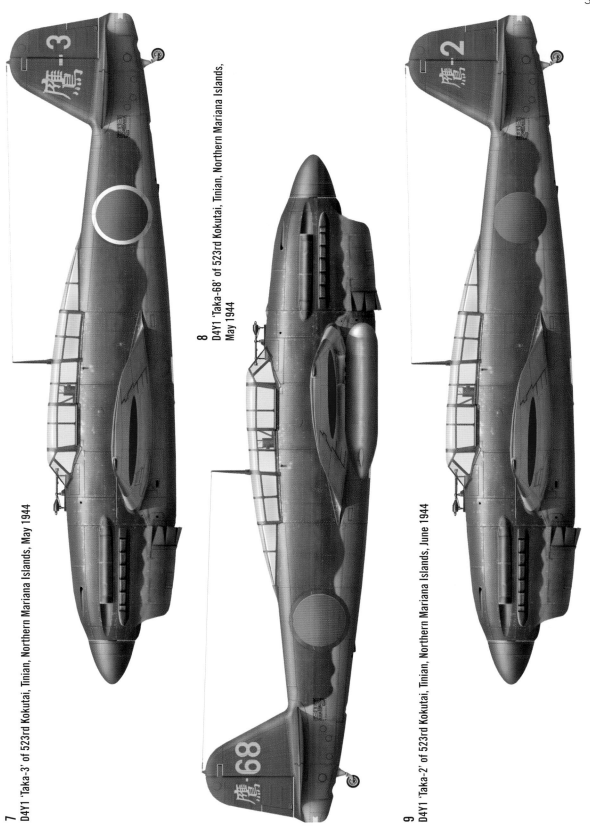

7
D4Y1 'Taka-3' of 523rd Kokutai, Tinian, Northern Mariana Islands, May 1944

8
D4Y1 'Taka-68' of 523rd Kokutai, Tinian, Northern Mariana Islands, May 1944

9
D4Y1 'Taka-2' of 523rd Kokutai, Tinian, Northern Mariana Islands, June 1944

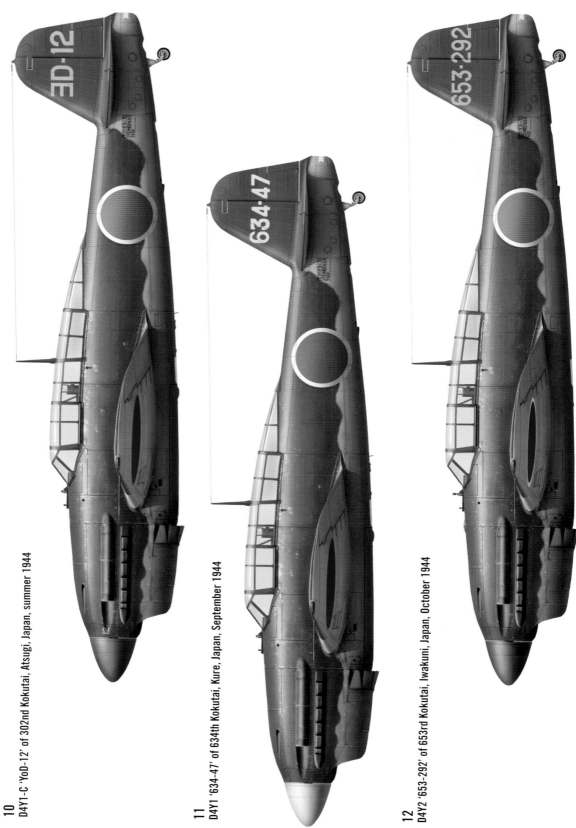

10
D4Y1-C 'YoD-12' of 302nd Kokutai, Atsugi, Japan, summer 1944

11
D4Y1 '634-47' of 634th Kokutai, Kure, Japan, September 1944

12
D4Y2 '653-292' of 653rd Kokutai, Iwakuni, Japan, October 1944

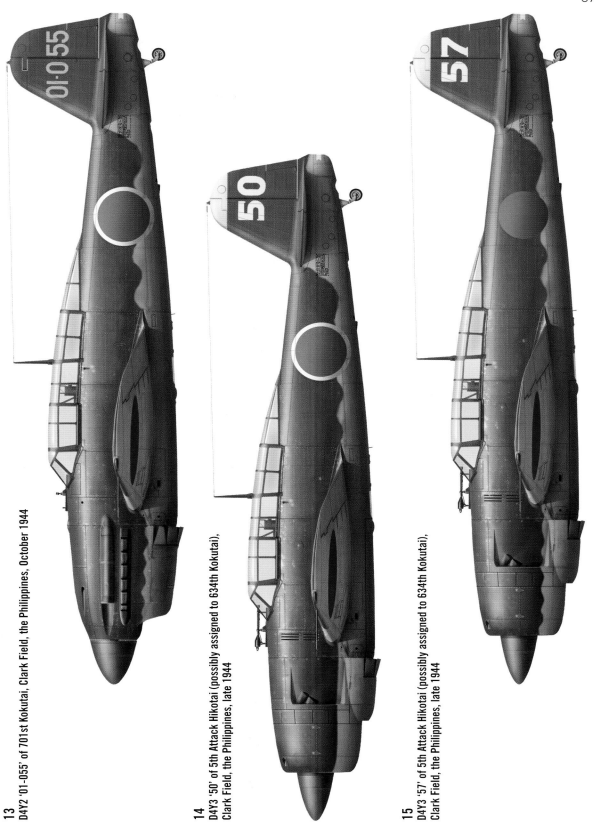

13
D4Y2 '01-055' of 701st Kokutai, Clark Field, the Philippines, October 1944

14
D4Y3 '50' of 5th Attack Hikotai (possibly assigned to 634th Kokutai),
Clark Field, the Philippines, late 1944

15
D4Y3 '57' of 5th Attack Hikotai (possibly assigned to 634th Kokutai),
Clark Field, the Philippines, late 1944

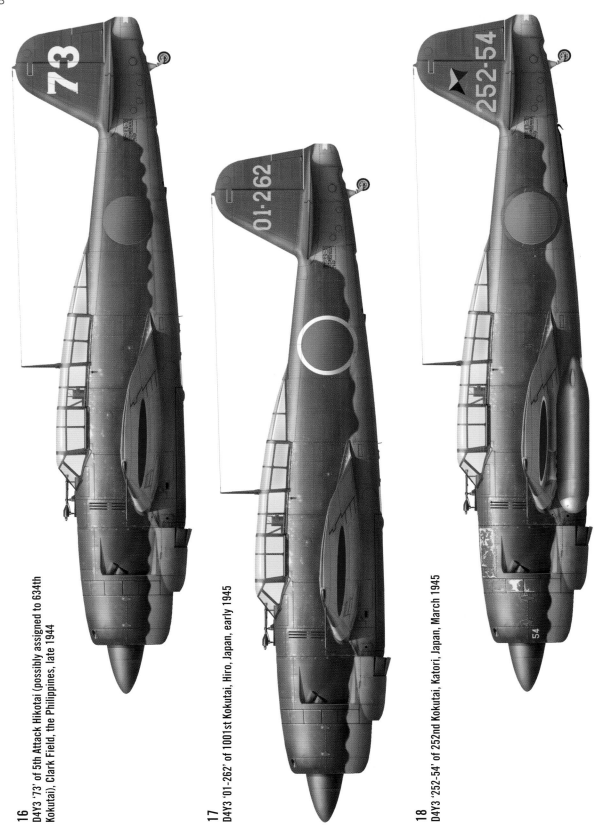

16
D4Y3 '73' of 5th Attack Hikotai (possibly assigned to 634th
Kokutai), Clark Field, the Philippines, late 1944

17
D4Y3 '01-262' of 1001st Kokutai, Hiro, Japan, early 1945

18
D4Y3 '252-54' of 252nd Kokutai, Katori, Japan, March 1945

According to Michael Wenger, editor of the English edition of *The Emperor's Sea Eagle*;

'Several Suisei from 1st Koku Sentai struck TG 58.2 just after noon. When the ships acquired the targets visually, there was considerable confusion on *Wasp*, and elsewhere, as to whether they were hostile or friendly, with the result that *Wasp* did not open up with its anti-aircraft batteries until just before the dive-bomber released. The aircraft approached in a glide from astern after breaking through overcast and was seen smoking as it retired, crashing some 12,000 yards off the starboard bow. The bomb landed just 50 ft off the port bow abreast frame No. 6, with splinters causing light damage to the hull and killing one sailor and wounding four others. In the meantime, two other Suisei attacked *Bunker Hill*, with both aircraft being shot down by that ship and other vessels in the screen.'

Returning to Abe's account;

'A third attack group from 2nd Koku Sentai [consisting of 49 aircraft, but no D4Y1s] took off at 1000 hrs from *Junyo*, *Hiyo* and *Ryuho*. However, this group returned and landed without detecting the enemy fleet at all, although enemy fighters shot down seven of their number. Thus, during the First Stage Attack, the IJNAF sent out a total of 241 aircraft, losing 135 with very little to show for the sacrifice.

'My bomber group from 2nd Koku Sentai led off the Second Stage Attack. At 1115 hrs, the following units totalling 50 aircraft took off; one division of dive-bombers from *Junyo* and two divisions from *Hiyo* [29 D3A2s in total], led by 20 escort fighters and three Tenzans. The attack force leader was Lt Yasunori Miyauchi from *Hiyo*. At 1145 hrs I departed with my lead division of nine Suisei, taking off later so as not to overrun the Type 99s. A second wave of 18 aircraft departed from 1st Koku Sentai at 1120 hrs. This later group returned without finding anything, most probably owing to the crews' poor navigational abilities.

'Having departed earlier, the Miyauchi group arrived at the supposed target area but no enemy fleet units appeared below. Having flown nearly 400 miles, there was now insufficient fuel to make the return flight to *Hiyo*. Accordingly, Miyauchi opted for a forced landing on Guam. However, just prior to landing, 30 F6Fs swooped down from the clouds and attacked Miyauchi from the rear, shooting down 26 aircraft.

'Meanwhile, prior to take-off. I was standing by on board *Junyo* wearing a flightsuit over my summer uniform. I carried nothing but a Navy-issue pistol in my trouser pocket and a pocket watch suspended around my neck. My division officer, Lt Junichi Kaga, walked up and reported, "Commander, the crews are waiting in line." Although I felt it was a bit early to man the aircraft, I still stood in front of the line, where my men then saluted me. I said nothing, as my excellent divisional officer and Ens Nakajima had given all the necessary last-minute instructions to my men already. Rear Admiral Jyojima's 2nd Koku Sentai staff instructed me to fly on to Guam after attacking the enemy task force, to refuel there, and thence return to *Junyo* the following day at a position which would be revealed to us at the time.

'Four days previously, US forces assaulted Saipan, which meant that our forces (and certainly our airfields on Guam) were now under threat and, accordingly, had lost a substantial portion of their counterattacking potential. Only 120 miles separated Saipan and Guam. Being somewhat accustomed to US practices, we should have expected the Americans to begin softening up our positions on Guam even before commencing the Saipan landings. Consequently, I was rather uneasy regarding our orders to land on Guam, much less on Saipan.

'Despite these concerns and misgivings, at 1145 hrs I lifted off from *Junyo*, leading nine Suisei dive-bombers and our accompanying escort of six Zero fighters under Lt Kenkichi Takasawa. I had not held a control stick in my hands for 40 days, and even on 10 May while in Suonada I flew for less than an hour. My ears were ringing, possibly from the engine noise, and I could not hear Nakajima's voice coming through the voice tube very clearly. Neither did he seem to understand my words at all. I seemed a bit unsteady on my legs and had an uneasy feeling as if I was simply riding in an aircraft flown by somebody else. Never had I experienced that kind of feeling since becoming a pilot (I did not realise it, but I was sick at that point). And just then CPO Kunio Kosemoto, piloting my second aeroplane, and Lt Kiyomi Iwai, my third Shotai-cho [section leader], turned back because their landing gear failed to retract, both aircraft aborting to Yap. Then, escort pilot CPO Shigenobu Manabe aborted due to engine trouble and returned to *Junyo*. Predictably, the strain placed on both men and machines of having not flown for 40 days had begun to take its toll.

'Flying just south of east and climbing up to 6000 m altitude, I put on my oxygen mask and breathed deeply. An hour later, Nakajima informed me through the voice tube that our little force had shrunk still further as Ens Hiroshi Tani's Suisei and three Zeroes were no longer there. I was deeply puzzled; had they dropped out because of engine trouble, or had they crashed into the sea due to hallucinations from oxygen starvation? My force in view was down to only six Suisei and two fighters.

'Continuing to fly for another hour, we arrived at the point where we expected to encounter the American fleet but I could not see anything owing to a hazy layer in the atmosphere at low altitude. Perhaps my own eyesight was failing. I inhaled more oxygen, and started a search of the surrounding area within an 80-mile radius, using our initial position as a centrepoint – this 80 miles being equivalent to four hours' steaming for the US fleet. However, strain though I might, I could not find anything below, still hoping that 80 miles might compensate for either navigation error on our part or movement by the enemy.

'With no targets, at 1340 hrs I finally gave up on the attack and focused instead on the flight ahead, shaping a course of 45° to Guam. At length, seeing Guam dimly in my mind through the haze at about two o'clock low, I descended gradually, keeping "three eyes open" to the surrounding expanse of sky. When the altimeter read 4000 m, Ens Nakajima shouted, "A big crowd of the enemy in our left front, Commander!" Just at that time, to the left underside of the engine cowling, I confirmed the presence of a US Task Force, all with their helms turned hard to port, cleaving glistening white wakes into the water below. There were more than 20 enemy vessels in a ring formation, with four aircraft carriers at the centre [it was TG 58.2, with the carriers *Bunker Hill*, *Wasp*, *Cabot* and USS *Monterey* (CVL-26)]. I gave the attack order and increased speed.

A bomb falls close to *Bunker Hill* on 19 June 1944, possibly during the raid by Lt Abe's six D4Y1s from *Junyo*. A tailless Suisei can be seen plummeting towards the sea to the left of the carrier, while another aircraft is diving on the vessel from the top right (*Michael Wenger Collection*)

'The Americans must have noticed us much earlier, as Grumman fighters were already climbing up to intercept us. We were in a very unsatisfactory position to deploy for the attack and had found the enemy almost too late. Now there was not a moment to lose. Lost seconds could mean certain death for us.

'I careened seaward in my attack dive through a heavy barrage of anti-aircraft fire. Even though my dive angle was far too shallow, I elected to release anyway, dropping a bomb into one of the big aircraft carriers in the centre. Incredibly, after flying past the enemy ships I found no one following me as I escaped from the hemisphere of anti-aircraft bursts. Nakajima later reported to me that he saw two fireballs in our rear as we dashed away from the target area.'

Analysing this strike with the benefit of post-war records, Michael Wenger noted, 'Abe's attack with just six aircraft was one of the more effective that day, with his unit mounting the assault at about 1426 hrs, attacking *Wasp* from its port quarter. The first bomb exploded on impact off the port bow, with shrapnel causing a small internal fire. Two more bombs fell off the starboard quarter, injuring two men on the flightdeck. Finally, a fourth bomb, possibly struck by anti-aircraft fire, detonated 300 ft above the flightdeck, littering *Wasp* with "bits of phosphorus that ignited when stepped on".'

It was also reported that the two Suisei targeting *Bunker Hill* during this attack scored two near misses, one of which killed three and wounded 75, started fires and temporarily knocked out the gasoline system in the hangar bay.

Having survived the ferocious anti-aircraft fire thrown up by the American ships, Abe now had to deal with US Navy fighters;

'While circling to collect what was left of my group, four aircraft approached, and I had already noticed that there was something peculiar about their silhouette. They were Grummans! I adjusted the propeller pitch, pushed my throttle to the stop and raced away from them. Fortunately, scattered clouds lay here and there at about 800 m altitude. Opposing these single-seat fighters, we certainly stood no chance, even with one-to-one odds. I still hoped to keep out of sight, but all too soon the small patches of clouds gave way to blue sky. "There's a Grumman, up and to the left rear, Commander!" shouted Nakajima. I again pushed the throttle forward, escaping into the nearest cloud. These Hellcat pilots were really tenacious, following us with a division of four aircraft.

'While fretting about our fuel situation, I heard Nakajima again, "Grummans, Grummans!" While I scrambled to configure our evasive manoeuvres so as to close on Guam, poor Nakajima was soon hoarse from screaming out his warnings. In turn, I was becoming disoriented in this fitful game of "Hellcat hide-and-seek", which by now had lasted for the best part of an hour. With daylight beginning to fail, I had no idea when our engine might stop and prompt me to dive into the sea, crying "Long reign the Emperor!" Thankfully, when I came out of the clouds there were no Grummans to harass us this time.

'I remember looking around and thinking, "Oh good, I've shaken off the Grummans now", when a land mass came into view for a fleeting moment. It was a small island, and I could barely make out what appeared to be a runway in its centre. I descended to 100 m, all the time flying closer and closer to the island. Then I saw another aircraft waggling its wings to identify itself as a friendly, flying east along the island's south coast. Although it was nearly sunset, it was just light enough for personnel on the ground to identify a red hinomaru on an approaching aircraft. If there were Japanese troops present perhaps they would wave handkerchiefs?

'Although I felt very anxious and apprehensive over the prospect of landing, I had almost no fuel left. So, while flying a circular pattern over

Rota airfield comes under attack by aircraft from *Yorktown* on 15 July 1944. Lt Abe landed here after attacking *Bunker Hill* the previous month during Operation *A-Go*, his Suisei being destroyed by Hellcats from VF-24 as it rolled down the runway (*Michael Wenger Collection*)

the northeast end of the island, I throttled back the engine and pushed my nose down toward the runway. The landing gear came down and locked without any problem; perhaps I could make a satisfactory landing. Just as I was on final approach, it felt as if someone had thrown pebbles and hit my flight helmet. "Oh no! I've landed in the middle of the enemy!" A hoarse Nakajima croaked, "Grummans, above and to the rear, Sir!" There was nothing to do now but land and run for cover.

'Hardly waiting for the aircraft to roll to a stop, Nakajima sprang from his rear seat and fled toward the woods on the right. Looking back, I thought that I saw a second Hellcat crashing. Yanking the voice tube from my flight helmet, I ripped loose my parachute harness and lap belt, and at last crawled out from the cockpit. A third Grumman flew away overhead, his engine roaring. I waited for the machine gun fire from the fourth fighter as I lay on my face, having run five or so metres into the bushes. This must have been the four-aeroplane division that had followed me so tenaciously earlier in the afternoon. After finishing their strafing runs, the four Grummans reversed course and dove in from the opposite direction, each aircraft appearing to drop a small bomb on my lone Suisei. Satisfied that they had probably destroyed my aircraft, they turned back toward their home base and flew out of sight. We had been exceedingly fortunate that their shooting and bombing skills were not so good.'

According to Michael Wenger, 'Abe and Nakajima's tormentors over Rota were almost certainly Hellcats from VF-24 embarked in the light carrier USS *Belleau Wood* (CVL-24). Initially, in the early evening hours, two divisions of VF-25 F6F-3s from USS *Cowpens* (CVL-25) strafed the airfield at 1847 hrs. Thirty minutes later, having launched from *Belleau Wood* at 1725 hrs, a fighter sweep of eight F6F-3s from VF-24 vectored toward Rota, broke through the towering cumulous at 2000 ft and attacked, destroying not only Lt Abe's Suisei as it rolled down the runway, but also a D3A2 in the dispersal area along the runway.'

Vice-Admiral Ozawa's 'out-of-range' tactics had kept 1st Koku Sentai safe from American air strikes on 19 June, but not from the threat posed by US Navy submarines. At 0909 hrs, his flagship *Taiho* was hit by a torpedo fired by USS *Albacore* (SS-218) just as the carrier was launching aircraft in the second attack wave. Many Japanese historians believe that D4Y1 pilot WO Sakio Komatsu spotted a second torpedo wake headed for *Taiho*. In a heroic act of self-sacrifice, he crashed his aircraft into the sea and onto the weapon in order to save the carrier from being hit again.

Despite Komatsu's bravery, the damage caused by the single torpedo strike was catastrophic as the ship's aviation fuel stores ignited after the weapon ruptured a tank. The resulting vapour explosion at 1532 hrs signalled *Taiho*'s demise, the carrier sinking at 1700 hrs. By then, Ozawa had transferred to the cruiser *Haguro*.

Shokaku also suffered a similar fate after being struck by three torpedoes launched by USS *Cavalla* (SS-244) at 1122 hrs while the ship's crew was refuelling and rearming aircraft. A veteran of the attack on Pearl Harbor, the carrier quickly sunk bow first with heavy loss of life.

The following day, Ozawa named *Zuikaku* as his new flagship. It was only then that he realised the comprehensive nature of the defeat 1st Koku

Sentai had suffered on 19 June, when it lost 330 aircraft and two carriers (the latter taking close to 3000 sailors with them when they sank).

At 1624 hrs on the 20th, while 220 miles southeast of the five surviving carriers of 1st Koku Sentai, TG 58.2 went on the offensive with the launching of more than 200 aircraft for a pre-dusk strike. Although 75 A6M5s were sent up in an effort to defend the fleeing vessels, a torpedo sunk *Hiyo* and bomb hits damaged the remaining four carriers to varying degrees. By the time the attack had ended, the IJNAF had just 35 serviceable aircraft embarked on the carriers. Only one of these was a D4Y1.

With the threat posed by Combined Fleet now neutralised, TG 58.2 continued on its offensive in the Central Pacific. Amongst the first targets it attacked following the Marianas clash was Iwo Jima on 24 June. A further 116 IJNAF aircraft were claimed as destroyed on this date, including 12 'Judys' sent out by a special combat detachment from the training/testing air group Yokosuka Kokutai known as the 'Hachiman Air Raid Unit', which had been deployed to Iwo Jima during Operation *A-Go*. The missions, mounted at dawn and dusk, were clinically dealt with by the Hellcat CAP. VF-2, flying from USS *Hornet* (CV-12), was credited with nine 'Judys' destroyed west of Iwo Jima at 0750 hrs, while VF-50, embarked in the light carrier USS *Bataan* (CVL-29), claimed three more 35 miles from the fleet at 1640 hrs. Although both strikes had had Zero-sen fighter escorts, none of the D4Y1s got within sight of the American carriers.

Having seized control of the Central Pacific, US forces in the region now took stock and made preparations for the invasion of the Philippines in the autumn of 1944. Taking full advantage of this lull in operations, the IJNAF tried to make good the losses it had suffered in June by forming new air groups in Japan and sending attrition replacements to established Kokutai. Amongst the aircraft reaching the frontline were the first D4Y2s.

Like all D4Y1s assigned to 523rd Kokutai in the Northern Mariana Islands in mid-1944, this aircraft has the Japanese kanji character symbolising the 'falcon' as part of its tail code – the air group was also known as the 'Falcon Corps'. 'Taka 2' was captured relatively intact by the US Marine Corps at Ushi Point airfield on 26 July 1944, the aircraft appearing to have been cannibalised by IJNAF groundcrew for parts rather than damaged by enemy action (*NARA*)

CHAPTER FOUR

FORMOSA AND THE PHILIPPINES

The observer keeps a watchful eye over the long nose of his brand new D4Y2 as the pilot taxis in at Iwakuni following a training mission in October 1944. The aircraft was part of 653rd Kokutai's 263rd Hikotai, which had been formed the previous month following a reorganisation of the air group's dive-bomber squadron under the newly adopted independent special hikotai system. Although the unit was principally equipped with B6N Tenzans, it also received seven D4Y2s to function in a reconnaissance role (*Tony Holmes Collection*)

With their once vast empire gradually shrinking in size, the Japanese made preparations for the defence of their Imperial remnants. Three plans were devised, known as *Sho-1* (defence of the Philippines), *Sho-2* (defence of Formosa and/or Okinawa) and *Sho-3* (defence of the Japanese Home Islands). The IJNAF would play a key role in these operations, with the vast majority of its aircraft now flying from land bases in all three locations.

By September 1944, American forces were less than 270 nautical miles southeast of Mindanao, the largest island in the southern Philippines, and the USAAF was able to target Japanese positions there using long-range bombers flying from recently captured airfields on Morotai, in the Maluku Islands. Troops under Gen Douglas MacArthur, Supreme Commander of Allied Forces in the Southwest Pacific Theater of Operations, had either overrun, isolated or bypassed all of the remaining Imperial Japanese Army strongholds in New Guinea and the Admiralty Islands.

Meanwhile, American naval forces under Admiral Chester W. Nimitz, Commander-in-Chief, US Pacific Fleet, and Commander-in-Chief, Pacific Ocean Areas, had advanced across the Central Pacific, capturing the Gilbert Islands, some of the Marshall Islands and most of the Mariana

Islands. With US Navy submarines taking a frightful toll of Japanese merchant shipping at the same time, it meant that the fortresses at Truk and Rabaul could be bypassed and left 'to wither on the vine', with no source of supplies and military capability.

The Allies were now ready for the next stage of the campaign against Japan. Senior officers in the US Navy wanted to seize the port of Amoy, on China's east coast, along with Taiwan (known as Formosa in the West throughout this period), while MacArthur was adamant that the Philippines had to be the priority. In July 1944, President Franklin D Roosevelt met with MacArthur and Nimitz in Hawaii, where the decision was made to invade the Philippines. The Joint Chiefs of Staff ordered MacArthur to plan an attack on the southern Philippines for the end of 1944, with Luzon to follow in early 1945.

Over the summer and autumn of 1944, in the wake of the invasion and seizure of the Marianas, aircraft flying from carriers of the US Navy's Third Fleet, commanded by Admiral William F Halsey, carried out several successful missions over the Philippines and found Japanese resistance to be decidedly lacking. Halsey then recommended a direct strike on Leyte ahead of other planned operations, with 20 October chosen as the date of the main landing – troops would actually come ashore 72 hours ahead of schedule.

Preliminary operations in preparation for the assault began early that same month, with the US Navy's fast carrier TF 38 under Halsey gathering off the southeastern coast of Formosa. It subsequently carried out a series of air strikes against airfields around Takao that were aimed at reducing the ability of the Japanese to fly reinforcements to the Philippines.

This early-build D4Y1-C, complete with a flat windscreen and no Type 2 Mark 1 optical gun/bombsight, was assigned to Yokosuka Kokutai as a crew trainer (*Tony Holmes Collection*)

Prior to the Formosa operation, clashes between US Navy fighters and Suisei units had been rare following the carnage of the First Battle of the Philippine Sea. The remnants of various land-based units, decimated in the battle for the Marianas, had fallen back on Yap, Palau and the southern Philippines. One of the units assigned Suisei for the reconnaissance role was 102nd Hikotai of 153rd Kokutai, which flew a small number of D4Y1-Cs in Western New Guinea from April to June 1944, and later in the Philippines after reorganisation from July 1944. It is possible that several of the 'Judys' downed by US Navy fighters in the autumn of 1944 came from this air group as the IJNAF attempted to keep tabs on the movement of the Pacific Fleet in the lead up to largescale operations in the Philippines from mid-October.

TF 38, consisting of nine fleet carriers and eight light carriers, had actually initiated a series of probing air strikes against Japanese airfields on Cebu and Negros Islands and in Manila as early as the second week of September. The paucity of D4Y1s in the region at this point is reflected in the fact that just two examples were claimed by US Navy fighters, although some of the 'Tonys' credited to Naval Aviators during these raids may have been 'Judys'. With both the IJAAF and the IJNAF fighting in the defence of the Philippines, confusion as to which type was being engaged would become increasingly commonplace.

On 10 October the Fast Carrier Task Force launched strikes on the Ryukyu Islands, which stretched from Kyushu in the northeast to Formosa in the southwest. Amongst the 23 aircraft claimed to have been shot down by US Navy pilots were two 'Judys' over Okinawa. Alarmed that this attack signalled the start of the US offensive, which IJN intelligence collected over previous weeks had indicated was imminent, the Combined Fleet Headquarters initiated the air component of *Sho-1* and *Sho-2* simultaneously on the morning of the 12th (the formal start of *Sho-1* for all Japanese forces was issued on 18 October).

Following a solitary day of attacks on the Ryukyu Islands, TF 38 switched its attention to Formosa. From 12 to 16 October, more than 1000 US Navy aircraft mounted a series of air raids on Japanese military installations on the island as a precursor to the amphibious invasion of Leyte on the 17th. Forty 'Judys' were claimed to have been destroyed by US Navy fighter squadrons during the operation, the dive-bombers primarily falling during attacks on TG 38.2.

Unsurprisingly, the IJNAF in particular had retaliated ferociously to the strikes on Formosa, with daily attacks flown against TG 38.2 between 10 and 16 October. During the afternoon of the 14th, for example, an estimated 25 D4Y1s from 5th Hikotai of 762nd Kokutai, which had been in Formosa since September, used cloud cover in an attempt to evade detection by CAPs and attack the carriers. Their strike was foiled by VF-18, however, as this extract from the unit's combat diary explains;

'Our 12 fighters on CAP this afternoon were returning to the ship [USS *Intrepid* (CV-11)] when "Jeep" Daniels, fighter director, vectored them out on a group of bogies nearing the screen. There were about 40 Judies and Tonies [the latter were also D4Y1s, as IJAAF and IJNAF units never flew together] bearing bombs and torpedoes, and they were caught completely by surprise when our fighters hit them from below [50 miles from TG 38.2]. We got 20, and lost none.'

Despite VF-18's outstanding tally of victories, a small number of D4Y1s managed to get through and drop bombs on USS *Hancock* (CV-19). Two were near misses and a third hit the forward port side gun tub without detonating on impact.

Following the implementation of *Sho-1*, the IJNAF hastily transferred a number of D4Y1/2-equipped air groups from Japan to airfields in the Philippines, where they came under the control of Second Air Fleet. The dive-bomber units known to have been despatched included hikotais successively assigned to 653rd, 701st, 752nd, 761st, 762nd and 763rd Kokutais. 141st Kokutai also flew a mixed fleet of D4Y1-Cs and C6N1s assigned to 3rd and 4th Hikotais. In addition, 601st Kokutai embarked fighters and bombers aboard the four carriers that took part in the Battle of Leyte Gulf. Seven D4Y2-Cs were among them, all assigned to *Zuikaku*.

By this stage of the war independent hikotai were being assigned to and transferred between kokutai as needed. The main Suisei-equipped units in the Philippines were 3rd, 5th, 102nd, 103rd and 105th Hikotais. By way of example, when it first arrived in the Philippines, 5th Hikotai was assigned to 752nd Kokutai, but later in October it was transferred to 701st Kokutai.

The most successful conventional attack undertaken by a land-based Suisei during the fighting in the Philippines took place shortly before

The most successful conventional attack mounted by a land-based Suisei during the fighting in the Philippines took place shortly before 1000 hrs on 24 October 1944 when two D4Y1s (possibly from 653rd Kokutai or 102nd or 103rd Attack Hikotais) emerged from low cloud cover above TG 38.3 and dived on their intended target – the light carrier USS *Princeton* (CVL-23). One aircraft scored a direct hit with a 250 kg bomb, while the second Suisei missed its intended target. Both D4Y1s then escaped unscathed. The single bomb started a large fire that eventually caused the carrier to explode (*Tony Holmes Collection*)

Vice Admiral Jisaburo Ozawa's First Mobile Force had been decimated during Operation *A-Go* in June 1944. During Operation *Sho-1* four months later, his carriers were so severely lacking in aircraft that their principal role in the defence of the Philippines was to act as a decoy for US carrier aircraft of Third Fleet (*Tony Holmes Collection*)

1000 hrs on 24 October and involved two D4Y1s from a force of 12 that had taken off singly from Mabalacat West, in central Luzon. Having escaped detection by the fighter CAP, the Suisei (possibly from 653rd Kokutai or 102nd or 103rd Attack Hikotais) emerged from low cloud cover above TG 38.3 and dived on their intended targets. One aircraft scored a direct hit on the light carrier USS *Princeton* (CVL-23) with a 250 kg bomb, while the second missed its intended target. Both Suisei managed to escape unscathed.

The bomb had hit the carrier between its elevators, penetrating the wooden flightdeck and passing through the hangar bay before exploding. Although the weapon caused minimal structural damage, the explosion had started a large fire, which rapidly spread because of burning aviation fuel. The conflagration raged for seven hours before a larger explosion at 1524 hrs sealed the carrier's fate. It was eventually scuttled at 1750 hrs, *Princeton* sinking 83 miles east-northeast of Pollilo Island, near Luzon.

Although the vast majority of the Suisei committed to *Sho-1* would operate from land bases in the Philippines, a modest number also participated in the IJN's final ever carrier action during the Second Battle of the Philippine Sea, also known as the Battle of Leyte Gulf. With the IJNAF having struggled to make good the grievous losses it had suffered off the Marianas four months earlier, this clash was almost a non-battle.

In theory, the four carriers of First Mobile Force could embark a total of 230 aircraft, but a lack of aeroplanes (most of the assigned air groups had been sent to Formosa earlier in October to support land-based units) and suitably qualified pilots meant that *Zuikaku*, *Zuiho*, *Chitose* and *Chiyoda* sailed with just 116 aircraft (assigned to 601st and 653rd Kokutais) embarked between them. As previously noted, the only Suisei included in their number were seven D4Y2-Cs on board *Zuikaku*.

Unlike in previous carrier clashes, where the IJN's once formidable 'flattops' had been Japan's premier maritime weapon, Vice Admiral Jisaburo Ozawa's First Mobile Force was to act primarily as a decoy for US carrier aircraft of Third Fleet, while nine battleships, 20 cruisers and more than 35 destroyers targeted the American invasion fleet in Leyte Gulf. This action was part of the overall *Sho-1* plan devised by the IJN to oppose the impending US landings in the Philippines. As with the elaborate plan that went so spectacularly wrong during the ill-fated defence of the Marianas, *Sho-1* was undone by the pre-emptive strikes by US carrier aircraft on airfields on Formosa, which were home to Japan's primary source of air support for the defence of the Philippines.

Once the day attacks on Formosa finally came to an end (20 October), Ozawa's First Mobile Force departed Oita Bight, off Kyushu, for the Philippines as part of *Sho-1*. The bulk of the IJN's battleships and cruisers left Brunei Bay two days later. Heading for the east coast of Luzon, Ozawa despatched D4Y2-C reconnaissance flights on 21 and 22 October in search of the US carriers, but no American ships were sighted until the 24th.

That morning, at 1145 hrs, *Zuiho*, *Chitose* and *Chiyoda* of First Mobile Force launched 53 aircraft on what proved to be virtually a suicide mission. Heading south, the IJNAF aeroplanes were quickly intercepted by Hellcats and virtually all of them shot down. The few survivors flew on to Clark Field, near Manila, as instructed by Ozawa prior to their departure. At 1155 hrs *Zuikaku* launched 29 aircraft (including two D4Y2-Cs) in the last offensive strike generated by a Japanese carrier. Aided by intermittent cloud cover, only 14 of these aeroplanes were lost to enemy action. After conducting a desultory attack on US ships, the survivors landed at Clark Field – 34 aircraft from First Mobile Force were now there. US Navy fighter units had claimed 270 victories (including land-based aeroplanes from both the IJNAF and IJAAF) on 24 October, of which six were identified as being 'Judys'.

The following day, Ozawa transferred most of his remaining aircraft to bases in the Philippines, with a solitary D4Y2-C being flown to Nichols Field at 0610 hrs to join the surviving aircraft from the First Mobile Force carriers. Lacking any fighter CAP, *Zuikaku*, *Zuiho*, *Chitose* and *Chiyoda* had all been sunk by US Navy aircraft by mid-afternoon during the Battle off Cape Engaño.

Although Suisei crews would increasingly become part of the growing cadre of Kamikaze Tokubetsu Kogekitai (Kamikaze Special Attack Corps), which officially began operations on 21 October, conventional dive-bomber units also continued to be sent to the Philippines through to year-end in a forlorn attempt to make good growing combat attrition. One such squadron was 3rd Hikotai, which sent 27 D4Y2s from Kokubu, in Kagoshima Prefecture on Kyushu, to join 701st Kokutai on 16 November. The unit routed to Mabalacat, via Taito airfield, on Formosa. It was forced to leave ten 'defective' Suisei behind here, before flying to the Philippines under the cover of darkness.

Amongst the pilots flying to Mabalacat with 3rd Hikotai was WO Shinsaku Yamakawa, who had previously seen action flying the D3A1. Assigned to the squadron when it was activated in the summer of 1944,

Newly delivered D4Y2s of 701st Kokutai are prepared for their next mission from Clark Field in late 1944. Aircraft parked in the open like this increasingly ran the risk of being strafed by marauding American fighters as the campaign in the Philippines swung in favour of the Allies. Deploying to Clark Field on 21 October, 701st Kokutai remained in-theatre through to 15 November, when it was withdrawn to Kokubu to re-equip (*PD-Japan-oldphoto*)

he recalls his experiences of fighting in the Philippines in the following extract from a post-war account;

'Upon our arrival, we came under the command of Lt Cdr Tamai, who, without delay, met with all crews to give them instructions for an attack on ships anchored off Leyte the following morning [18 November]. However, just before dawn, ready for the mission, a large-scale air raid by more than 300 aircraft – the most I had ever seen in my life – reduced all the Suisei to little more than ashes.

'"Cancel today's attacks", said Lt Cdr Tamai, leaving me mortified beyond words. I could not understand why he hadn't let me take off before the air raid. And how had the enemy aircraft known to target Mabalacat just hours after we had flown in from Taito? I was soon told that there was a mountain nicknamed "Manila Fuji" [Mount Arayat] to the east of Clark Field from where Philippino guerillas working with the US armed forces spotted all aircraft movements, and then radioed detailed reports to the USAAF. That evening, the destroyed Suisei were replaced with examples hastily flown in from Kyushu.

'Every day, we searched for enemy ships while flying from an airfield that was at risk of being attacked by air strikes. We could not find the enemy's aircraft carriers, however. We remained on alert, ready to attack such vessels should they be found. In the meantime, the squadron was kept busy attacking convoys of transport ships sailing in Leyte Gulf on a near-daily basis. We would usually send up a four-aeroplane formation on such missions, and only one or two aeroplanes would return.

'Shortly after arriving in the Philippines, the base commander called for volunteers to form a Special Attack [kamikaze] Unit, and a number of the younger aircrew left the squadron. The rest of us kept on flying missions over Leyte Gulf.

'On 8 December, it was decided that four aeroplanes under the command of Lt Yonosuke Iguchi would launch an attack on the convoys offshore Dulag and Tacloban, again within the Leyte Gulf. Two aeroplanes of the 3rd Attack Squadron would be joined by two Suisei from the 5th Attack Squadron. After receiving formal instructions, we boarded the aircraft – I flew with Lt Iguchi, who served as my navigator. Each Suisei was armed with a single 500 kg bomb. We circled above the airfield once in the air, before gradually climbing as we headed southeast for Leyte Gulf.

'After almost 20 minutes, Manila City became visible – red roofs and white walls. Gradually, I ascended higher, but due to the weight of the 500 kg bomb, I could not quite attain the altitude I desired. After crossing Luzon and spotting Samar Island to our left, the clouds grew increasingly thick. I momentarily hesitated while deciding whether I should go above or below them, before deciding to go above. When I looked down at the cumulonimbus clouds from above, they were as beautiful as white cotton or snow. When we reached an altitude of 5000 m, the clouds ahead of us appeared to be even higher. We were not carrying oxygen that day, which meant we could not go any higher. We would have to ascend. There was no break in the clouds, even beneath them.

'It had been about two hours since we had taken off and, approximately 30 minutes from now, we would see Leyte Gulf. Although I knew it was unreasonable to do so [without oxygen], I started climbing again. My body felt "dull", and I began gasping. I continued to climb, however, telling myself, "Just a little more. Hang in there". Finally, at an altitude of 6000 m, a break in the clouds appeared before us. I hurriedly led the Suisei down to a lower altitude, at which point I saw an island off to the left. I took out my map and compared it to what I saw. It looked just like Leyte Island.

'"How much longer will it take until we reach Leyte Gulf?", I asked Lt Iguchi. "Thirty minutes", he replied. "But this is Leyte Island", I countered. For the life of me, I thought what I could see was Leyte Island, with Leyte Gulf directly ahead of us. Yet the timing was too soon.

'At an altitude of 5000 m, all four aircraft stuck closely together. The island that I saw on the right-hand side, when compared to the one on the map, was unmistakably Cebu.

'"Lt Iguchi, Leyte Gulf is ahead of us", I informed him. Maybe the Lieutenant had lost his self-confidence while flying over the clouds. He replied with a brief "I see".

'We rapidly approached the gulf. There were countless convoys, totalling between 80 and 90 ships, heading in both directions between Tacloban and Dulag. I had heard that Grumman F6F and Lockheed P-38 fighters were constantly patrolling the skies over Leyte, so we proceeded on high alert, but could not see any enemy aeroplanes.

'Thinking the enemy too had loosened their guard in this atrocious weather, we began our approach to the target. No high-angle [anti-aircraft artillery] shells came up at all, and there were a lot of targets. With a broad,

This still taken from gun camera footage retrieved from a USAAF P-38 Lightning shows an attack on an unsuspecting D4Y2 heading for US naval targets in Leyte Gulf. Although this drop-tank-equipped aircraft almost certainly had an observer in the rear cockpit, he has failed to engage the American fighter with his flexibly-mounted 13 mm Type 2 machine gun (*NARA*)

satisfied smile, I formed the four aircraft up into an attack formation – a charging battle formation. At that very moment, our engine shook intensely and ran to idle. It had stopped.

'I was startled for a moment. I had been using the right drop tank, which was hanging below the wing, up until now. It was only then that I noticed it was empty. The contents of the left drop tank had already been used up, and the tank discarded. So, when I hurriedly switched the petcock and pushed the hand pump three or four times, the engine shuddered and then roared back into life.

'Moments later I radioed, "I'm breaking formation", glancing behind me as I made the transmission. The remaining three Suisei were behind, along with a fourth machine! When did our numbers increase by one, the new aircraft joining without anyone noticing? When I looked at the new arrival more closely, I discovered that it was in fact a twin-boom P-38.

'This was the first time I had seen the enemy aeroplane that had been tormenting my contemporaries on an everyday basis since the Americans invaded the Philippines.

'"Lt Iguchi, it's a P-38!" I anxiously called over the radio. He had no combat experience, which meant he was so fixated with seeing the enemy's great fleet of ships that he had forgotten to keep a lookout behind us for fighters. As the P-38 drew nearer, I could clearly see its twin booms. It somehow felt like a monster was swooping down on me.

'I immediately banked the nose of our aircraft to the left, facing the fleet off the coast of Tacloban, before bunting down into a dive. The P-38 followed me, the pilot using his engine overboost, or war emergency power to remain on my tail. He quickly opened fire, and Lt Iguchi replied with his rear, flexibly-mounted machine gun. I turned my eyes away from the fleet and looked behind me. A twin-boom monster approached within an arm's reach, allowing me to see the triumphant face of the enemy pilot.

'The P-38 remained stuck to our tail, despite my attempt to escape by diving away. During my previous engagements with Hellcats, I had found that I could easily escape the Grumman fighter by pushing the Suisei over into a nosedive. However, the Lockheed was proving to be an entirely different kind of foe.

'I banked tightly to the right with all my might, at which point a large black object soared overhead – this was the empty drop tank that had been hanging beneath the right wing. I then set my sights on an enemy transport vessel sailing in the water below us. Although the P-38 pilot tried to stay with me through this violent manoeuvre, the American fighter was soon forced to break off the pursuit.

'Still the ships' guns remained silent. Perhaps the gunners were engrossed in the aerial battle taking place above them. My beloved Suisei headed for the target at an incredible rate – "2000 m altitude", I shouted, then "1000 m altitude". The enemy ships rapidly filled my windscreen, their details magnified in my sighting device. Indeed, the surface of the water appeared to be full of ships. When they finally started shooting, in panic, it was too late.

'I pulled the bomb release lever in the cockpit and the 500 kg weapon fell away from the centreline bomb-bay, generating a distinctive howl as it went. Moments later, I spotted a pillar of flames from my target, which was soon obscured by thick smoke [it is possible that Yamakawa hit USS *LCI(L)-684*, as the 389-ton Landing Craft Infantry sank off Samar after being attacked on this date].

'"It's a direct hit!" exclaimed Lt Iguchi.

'With the bomb gone, I raced across the gulf just above the water. In fact, I was so low that I thought I might clip a ship's mast. At that height, however, the gunners on board the vessels would not have had the time to aim at us before we had flashed past.

'Scanning the sky ahead, I spotted four Grummans waiting for us. To the left of them was a thick bank of cloud.

'"It's going to be fine", I assured Lt Iguchi, who did not respond.

'It was unfortunate that I had no fixed gun (the weapon had been damaged during a raid on Mabalacat the previous day), as when I pulled up with a mighty effort, one of the Grummans filled my windscreen. Its pilot then made a wide turn in order to sneak in behind me. At that moment, I banked the Suisei to port and raced for the clouds, as did the Grumman after its pilot violently reversed his turn.

'As I raced for the safety of the "wall of clouds", the Grumman pilot fired a warning shot of red tracer across the front of my aircraft. He was too late, however, and the Suisei plunged unscathed into the cloud cover.

'I mistakenly thought I could make good my escape by remaining within the clouds. The aeroplane, however, was violently tossed up, down, left and right, preventing me from estimating whether sufficient time had passed to secure our escape, or to ascertain exactly where we were. Lt Iguchi remained silent throughout this period, seemingly exhausted from his first taste of combat.

'The Suisei continued to be hurled vertically and horizontally for a full 20 minutes as we passed through 6000 m. Then, suddenly, we flew out of the clouds and into clear skies, the ocean stretching out in front of us.

'"Thank goodness!" I exclaimed over the intercom.

'When I turned my head to check on Lt Iguchi, I saw that his face was stained with blood.

'"What's the matter?' I enquired. "Were you hit?"

'"No", he replied. "When you suddenly pushed over into a nosedive, I was in the middle of shooting at the P-38. This abrupt manoeuvre caused me to knock my face on the gun." He then apologised for not being able to keep a better lookout behind the aircraft after hitting his face.

'We eventually landed back at Mabalacat, having seen nothing more of the rest of our formation after being bounced by the lone P-38. Once home, we discovered that the other Suisei had also successfully attacked the enemy ships, survived being intercepted by the Grummans after taking cover in the same cloud bank as Lt Iguchi and I, and made it safely back to base.'

Conventional attacks such as this one by 701st Kokutai were very much a rarity by December 1944, as kamikaze operations were now the norm, rather than the exception. Even they had run their course by mid-January 1945, with both the IJNAF and the IJAAF admitting defeat in the Philippines. On the ground, however, pockets of resistance remained until war's end in August 1945.

CHAPTER FIVE

KAMIKAZES

One of the IJNAF's most effective tokko aircraft, the D4Y could carry a 1764-lb bomb in a suicide role. This particular D4Y3, flown by Lt(jg) Tadashi Tanabe (pilot) and Ens Taro Kudo of the 4th Kamikaze Special Attack Unit's Katori-tai (drawn from 3rd Attack Hikotai of 701st Kokutai), was photographed moments before it hit the deck of USS *Essex* on 25 November 1944. One of two kamikazes that targeted the ship, this aircraft was the only one to succeed in its mission, striking the carrier's flightdeck. The resulting explosion started a fire that killed 15 and wounded 44 (*NARA*)

The ineffectiveness of conventional air attacks on US Navy surface ships, particularly heavily defended targets like carrier task groups, forced the Japanese to re-evaluate their tactics in the autumn of 1944. The solution they arrived at was simple – crash their aircraft into Allied vessels. This notion of self-sacrifice fitted well within the Japanese warrior psyche. Indeed, the traditions of the Samurai warrior class in premodern times saw ritual disembowelment (i.e. 'seppuku', or as a vulgar, vernacular term, 'hara-kiri') as a virtuous act to avoid dishonour.

There was a strong ethos which glorified death in battle, and giving one's life for emperor and nation in the Japanese armed forces in modern (i.e. post-feudal) times. The majority of Japanese were adherents of Shinto and Buddhist religious beliefs. These religions do not impose the same strict prohibition against suicide as does Christian tradition.

Starting in the 1930s, there had been a growing trend toward strict prohibition against being captured alive by the enemy. This had become institutionalised by the start of the Pacific War. Surrender was simply not an option, which left either victory or death.

In the context of aerial warfare, any pilot who found himself over enemy territory mortally wounded or in an aeroplane too damaged to return to friendly territory was expected to deliberately crash into the enemy in an act known as 'jibaku' ('self-explode', or more colloquially, 'self-destruct') in Japanese airman jargon. This was evident from the very first day of the

Pacific War when Lt Fusata Iida, a fighter squadron leader in the attack on Pearl Harbor, had his fuel tank ruptured. Deciding he would not have enough fuel left to return to his carrier, he deliberately crashed his Zero-sen into a building on the US Naval Air Station at Kaneohe Bay, on Oahu.

So, with such psychology already permeating Japan's air forces, crossing the line to deliberately organised suicide sorties once the war situation turned grave was not so shocking. Such tactics proved terrifying to the Allied sailors subjected to them, however, and they also brought immediate results. The US Navy, in particular, was forced to adapt its tactics and operations, and deploy new weapons to counter the threat.

While American defences destroyed most kamikazes before they had a chance to strike their intended targets, these attacks, nevertheless, inflicted significant losses. More than 400 ships and craft were struck by kamikazes, of which 47 were sunk. Personnel casualties were also horrendous with 6190 killed and 8760 wounded. Ultimately, however, the kamikazes were unsuccessful.

As previously noted, although a policy of deliberately crashing an aircraft into a target was not officially adopted until late 1944, there were documented instances before then of Japanese pilots aiming their aircraft at US Navy ships. Sometimes, this was the result of a pilot deciding to do the maximum amount of damage with a crippled aircraft, and on other occasions it appeared to be deliberate from the start.

These suicide attacks, known as tai-atari (body-crashing), were very much the exception to the rule during the early stages of the conflict in the Pacific. At the start of the war, the IJNAF's pilots were the best-trained naval aviators in the world. The carrier pilots were the cream of the crop, and showed themselves to be formidable adversaries. From Pearl Harbor to the Indian Ocean and then in the carrier battles of Coral Sea and Midway, they were renowned for their prowess. Clinical in their employment of the bomb and the torpedo, naval aviators had no need to resort to kamikaze tactics. And although Midway was a disaster from the standpoint that four of the IJN's fleet carriers were sunk, aircrew losses were not yet crippling.

This changed during the fighting for Guadalcanal, which was a grinding six-month battle of attrition. There were two carrier clashes during the campaign, and the second one in October 1942 – the Battle of Santa Cruz – was a Pyrrhic victory, with Japanese aircrew losses being worse than at Midway. Just as alarming, some 1100 naval aircraft were lost during the entire campaign, along with most of their highly trained crews. This was followed by a prolonged attempt during much of 1943 to slow the American advance up the Solomon Islands, this fighting featuring a constant series of aerial battles. The net result was to gut the IJNAF's cadre of highly trained aircrew.

The effect of this was dramatically demonstrated in June 1944 in the largest carrier action of the war. As detailed in the previous chapter, during the First Battle of the Philippine Sea, the IJN gathered together nine carriers, with 430 embarked aircraft. This carefully husbanded force was committed against the American invasion of the Mariana Islands. In the clash that ensued, the IJN had three carriers sunk and the IJNAF lost almost 400 aircraft in what proved to be one of the most one-sided battles of World War 2. Most disturbingly for the IJN, its greatest massing of

A group shot of airmen from the 13th Flight Specialist Reserve Students class assigned to 210th Kokutai at Meiji, in Aichi Prefecture on Honshu, in March 1945. They are posing in front of well-weathered D4Y3 '210-215' – at the time this photograph was taken, the air group possessed 23 D4Y3 dive-bombers, five D4Y2-S nightfighters and 27 D4Y1/2-C reconnaissance aircraft. Of the six men in flight gear shown here, four were killed in action during the Okinawa campaign (*Tony Holmes Collection*)

carrier air power resulted in a total of just three US Navy ships being slightly damaged and none sunk. In this battle, 60 IJNAF aircraft made bombing attacks and scored only five hits or near misses. None of these caused major damage.

To put it simply, conventional air attacks by IJNAF torpedo- and dive-bombers had become increasingly ineffective. By one detailed accounting, in the first six months of 1944, 315 IJNAF aircraft survived fighter interception to attack various US Navy ships. Of these, a further 106 were shot down by anti-aircraft fire. Having escaped the CAP and avoided being struck by a barrage of defensive fire, just 10 per cent of aircraft scored a hit on their intended target. Typically, they would usually inflict only superficial damage.

When engaging the US Navy's Fast Carrier Task Force between November 1943 and June 1944, less than 5 per cent of aircraft hit a target in daylight attacks and just over 2 per cent were successful at night. In daylight, 195 aircraft had made attacks and 40 per cent of them had been destroyed by anti-aircraft fire.

Against this backdrop, the examination of possible suicide tactics began to gain traction. Even before the debacle of the First Battle of the Philippine Sea, there had been discussions in 1943 amongst the IJNAF's leadership about adopting suicide tactics. By August 1944, it was widely accepted that only suicide operations could change the course of the war, and eight weeks later, senior naval officers were openly discussing forming Tokubetsu Kogeki (Special Attack), abbreviated to tokko, units to fly serviceable, bomb-laden aircraft and crash them into an enemy ship. The term 'Kamikaze' (Divine Wind) was the name first chosen by the IJNAF for a specific series of Special Attack units. Allied intelligence picked up on the name, and it came to be used as a generic term referring to all such Japanese suicide attacks.

The man who turned the theory of Special Attacks into formal action was Vice Admiral Takijiro Onishi (soon to be appointed commander of 1st Air Fleet in the Philippines). He requested approval from the Chief of the Naval General Staff to form a tokko unit to carry out suicide strikes on the US Navy's Pacific Fleet.

Although initially opposed to the idea of such attacks when first briefed on them, Onishi had quickly realised that conventional attacks had little chance of success against the overwhelming firepower of the US forces being massed for the imminent invasion of the Philippines. It was decided that the best way to inflict maximum damage on the enemy forces approaching Japan was to get the poorly trained IJNAF and IJAAF pilots to crash their aircraft into their targets, thus essentially becoming guided bombs.

On the surface, the kamikaze appeared to be a formidable weapon, and the formal adoption of the suicide attack was an extraordinary opportunity to turn the course of the war. The basis for its effectiveness was its sophisticated guidance system – a human pilot with the ability to instantaneously adjust to changing situations and guide his aircraft to the target. The pilot could theoretically select the most valuable ship for attack, and then fly his aircraft into its most vulnerable part. Once at the target, the pilot was trained to release his bomb to cause additional damage, before his aircraft became a multi-ton projectile with the added destructive power of any unused fuel still on board.

The kamikaze would make their debut towards the end of the series of engagements known collectively as the Battle of Leyte Gulf. These had gone so disastrously wrong for the Japanese that they spelled the end of the IJN as an effective fighting force. Indeed, by the time the battle had come to its conclusion, the kamikaze constituted Japan's most viable option for responding to the invasion of Leyte and future American targets in the Philippines, and beyond.

The following US Navy report from the summer of 1945 on the kamikaze threat detailed the evolution of the tactics and techniques employed by the suicide attackers that inflicted so much damage on Allied ships during the final ten months of the war in the Pacific;

'Japanese suicide tactics have improved in several respects since their inauguration during the Philippines campaign. Most important of the enemy changes in tactics are the following;

1. Highly concentrated attacks on DD [destroyer] radar picket stations.
2. Increased coordination during multiple attacks.
3. Inauguration of night attacks and increased emphasis on attacks at dawn and dusk.
4. Use of special suicide equipment, such as the "Baka" [Yokosuka MXY7 Ohka].

'In the light of information obtained from ships' description of enemy attacks since the occupation of the Philippines, Japanese suicide tactics are summarised as follows;

'The first attacks were made in the daytime exclusively. These attacks were directed, chiefly, and were concentrated around the noon hour when carriers were engaged in launching new strikes or receiving returning planes. Because attrition as a result of air cover made daytime attacks too costly, the enemy changed to twilight attacks, with emphasis being placed on those at dusk. There were no suicide attacks in the Philippines between 2100 hrs and 0400 hrs.

'At Iwo Jima in February [1945] the only suicide attacks occurred between 1700 hrs and 2000 hrs. In March, on the other hand, when attacks occurred in the Kyushu–Okinawa area, nearly all firing at enemy aircraft was done at dawn. However, there were several attacks in the afternoon, and at least six between midnight and 0400 hrs. During the occupation of Okinawa in April, approximately 80 per cent of the attacks occurred between 1400 hrs and 1900 hrs. The other peak period was from 0600 hrs to 0900 hrs, and a few raids occurred at noon. In May, attacks were made almost exclusively at dawn and dusk. There is a trend toward more night attacks, and an increase in this type may be expected.

'A Japanese Suicide Manual outlining such procedures recommends that planes take off in the following order – first the guide planes, then the intermediate escort force, the direct escort force and, finally, the suicide force. The rendezvous is carried out with the suicide planes as the nucleus over a point near the airfield of departure. If enemy planes are in the area, the Jap force is advised to take off especially rapidly and fly at extremely low altitude to a rendezvous point.

'After the rendezvous, the attack force commander orders the advance. "The route of advance will by all means avoid interception by enemy fighters", according to the Japanese instruction manual, which continues, "At times it will be better to pick detours so as to make a surprise raid on the enemy. While advancing, give due regard to general atmospheric conditions, making every effort to take advantage of local weather conditions, that is, clouds, sun and wind direction. This will be especially true in daylight and surprise attacks.

'"In the advance, the attack force commander will determine the altitude and speed of the advance with due regard for the performance of the suicide and escort planes. Both forces must guard against any separation at all during the advance. This applies particularly in case of poor weather and atmospheric conditions.

'"The formation for the advance will depend on conditions, particularly on the attack method (strong raid, surprise raid, etc.), on the strength used and on the disposition of the enemy. It is particularly advantageous to deceive the enemy by adopting formations and manoeuvres which resemble those of his carrier-borne aircraft."

'The document advocated as a rule of thumb that for "strong" raids a high-speed, high-altitude approach be made, and that for a "surprise" raid an extremely low-altitude approach be made.

'Because attack groups often are intercepted and broken up before reaching their objectives, and because the enemy frequently lacks aircraft in sufficient quantity and quality to comply with the formal approach doctrines outlined in the Japanese manual, enemy approach tactics as witnessed by our own planes and ships are given here;

'**Avoiding Interception by CAP** – since the only mission of suicide pilots is to crash into US naval vessels, they make every effort to avoid our fighter cover. They fly very high – above 20,000 ft – or very low. Camouflage is designed to make the planes difficult to detect either from above or below. When intercepted by our fighters, the formations break up and planes evade independently, making best use of the sun and cloud cover. Cloud cover, especially, makes interception by CAP difficult. When about ten miles from the ships to be attacked, planes making a high-level approach go into a 20–30-degree power glide. Cloud conditions generally govern the altitude of approach – the higher the clouds the higher the approach. Concealment by flying low over land is a favourite tactic, and the enemy may be expected to take every possible advantage of land masses in the future.

'That the enemy's effort to avoid CAP has not been entirely satisfactory has been indicated by his trend toward twilight attacks. In these, his tendency is to approach from the direction of the dark horizon. In night attacks, the approach is usually with the ship silhouetted against the moon.

'**Avoiding Radar Detection** – to hamper fighter direction and target acquisition, the enemy has used weaknesses in our search radars to excellent advantage. Many attacks are made from the direction of the nearest land, against which the target is lost on radar screens. During a high-altitude approach, enemy planes pass through radar null areas, and during low-level approaches they pass under the radar horizon.

'Frequently, suiciders trail in the shadow of the IFF [Identification Friend or Foe transponder] of our planes returning to their bases. In several instances, enemy aircraft have been suspected of using IFF codes similar to that used by our own aircraft. During twilight and night attacks, "Window" or "Phantoms" are employed to confuse our radar screens, and have been more effective against our nightfighters than our ships.

'Surprise is effected occasionally by splitting up into several small groups and approaching from different altitudes and bearings. One or two groups usually are picked up, but another may slip through undetected.

'**Avoiding Visual Detection** – besides fighter and radar detection, the enemy seeks to make the visual detection problem difficult. Best use is made of clouds, sun, land background, the dark horizon at dawn and dusk and other natural phenomena.

'After reaching attack position – effective AA gun range – enemy planes continue tactics directed at effecting surprise and, in addition, at complicating the fire control problem.

'The most obvious change since the Philippines campaign has been the increase in multiple, coordinated attacks which saturate the AA defence of ships under attack. This has been especially characteristic of attacks against radar picket stations.

'The Japanese Suicide Manual states that, "The basis for success in attack is getting lined up on the target and keeping on it. The suicide force commander and his men will calmly, cleverly, and rapidly, locate their targets, then make a systematic attack run. As soon as the attack targets are discovered, the pilots will first pull the fuse-arming vane release handle and

A tokko pilot contemplates his fate whilst sat in the cockpit of a D4Y3 from an unidentified unit. Six slits on the side of the fuselage ahead of the engine firewall confirm that this Suisei is indeed a radial-engined Model 33. The small round hole above the slits is for gas exhaust venting from the two cowl-mounted 7.7 mm Type 97 machine guns. The unusual windscreen and Type 2 Mark 1 optical gun/bombsight arrangement seen on most Suisei is clearly visible here. Note the cap cover fitted to the front of gun/bombsight is in the open position (*Tony Holmes Collection*) then close the attack on the enemy by diving down on him at full speed, following him like a whirlwind, and countering every move he makes. At this time every effort must be made to avoid losses from the enemy CAP and AA barrage by appropriate manoeuvres.

'"The final run-in will differ according to conditions, particularly the types of plane, weather, atmospheric conditions, etc. – however, either a steep dive or an extreme low-altitude final run-in will be used. In all circumstances, the right points for beginning the attack run and final run-in must be chosen so as to have the desired momentum at the time of collision.

'"The final run-in for a steep-diving attack will differ with the type of plane. However, the approach to the enemy will be at high altitude, then altitude and speed will be successively adjusted (this varies with the situation, but it will be best to adjust the speed twice, at 6700 yds and 4500 yds). Take into consideration the speed and altitude at the commencement of the final run-in, and care must be taken so that the diving angle is neither too steep nor too shallow.

'"Although generally the steep diving attack method is employed, precautions must be taken because acceleration during the attack run causes the diving angle and maintenance of speed to be unsatisfactory at the point of beginning the final run-in, thus resulting in an inability to collide with the ship.

'"In the final run-in for a low-level horizontal attack, the enemy will be approached at high altitude. Then, by rapid plane manoeuvres, while speed and altitude are successively adjusted, arrive at the point for beginning the attack run. Either a diving collision or a horizontal collision attack run will be made. At this time speed will be maintained and the right point for beginning the attack run will be selected. At the time of the collision, sufficient colliding power must be maintained.

'"Just before the collision, the elevator control must be sufficiently pressed forward to allow for the increase in speed. It is essential at this time not to miss the target because of shutting one's eyes for a moment."

'Japanese attack-run tactics as reported by ships include the following;

'Diving out of the clouds or sun at angles of 20° to 45° from altitudes of 3000 ft to 6000 ft and from ranges of 3000 yds to 6000 yds.

'Weaving low on the water until within 1000 yds of ship, then zooming up to 1500 ft, doing a wingover and crashing onto ship's deck or superstructure.

'Weaving low on the water and continuing torpedo-type run into side of ship or superstructure (amphibious and other lightly armoured ships are the usual targets of this type of attack).

'Attempting to make a topside crash from dead astern or dead ahead.

'A low approach past the bow or stern of the target, then a sharp vertical turn into the target's bridge.

'Making radical manoeuvres in some cases but, as a general rule, evading slightly or not at all. Ships report evasive tactics, usually of a mild sort, in 20 per cent of the known cases during the period February–May, as compared with 41 per cent in the Philippines.

'Carriers and troop transports have been given first priority as targets by Japanese suicide doctrine. As a result of their exposed positions while on picket duty, however, and the difficulty of evading fighters under their control, destroyers have been subject to attack more frequently than any other type of ship during the period February–May.

'It should be pointed out that when a carrier was in formation, it was almost invariably singled out for attack. Landing craft were taken under attack chiefly when they were attached to picket stations.

'When damaged by AA fire or harassed by our planes, suiciders selected targets of opportunity. Once hit, a ship was likely to be attacked by other planes seeking to finish it off.

'Heavy ships have not been attacked as frequently as in the Philippines campaign. This is probably a result of the enemy's realisation that battleships and cruisers are able to defend themselves with greater effectiveness and are less vulnerable to critical damage than lighter ships.

'According to Japanese doctrine, "The collision point will vary with the type of plane, kind of target and its size and speed, but in the event of a steep diving collision, it will be on the deck, amidships if possible, between the stack and the bridge, and for carriers, at the elevators. In the case of an extreme low-altitude horizontal collision, the best point will generally be amidships slightly above the water line."

'In many cases the collision point has been the bridge itself. Crashes into the hull have been confined largely to destroyers and other lightly armoured ships. When attacking aircraft carriers, suicide pilots often aim for planes spotted on the deck.'

The exact number of suicide attackers sent against Allied ships from October 1944 until the end of the war is difficult to determine with certainty. An accepted source states that 3913 Japanese aircrew died conducting some 3000 kamikaze missions. This included 2525 IJNAF personnel. Of these 3000 missions, only one-third reached the point where they conducted an attack on a ship. If the aircraft got to this point, it had about a 36 per cent chance of success. Some 367 kamikazes hit their target or gained a near miss close enough to cause damage. In total, each kamikaze aircraft had about a 9.4 per cent chance of hitting a target, and if it did, it caused an average of 40 casualties.

The cost to the US Navy and its Allies was 66 ships or craft sunk or never repaired and almost 400 damaged in some measure. Of the ships or craft that never returned to service, only 47 were sunk outright. Coming up with personnel casualties is difficult, but a figure of approximately 16,000 is generally accepted as accurate. This total includes 6190 killed and 8760 wounded. According to official US Navy records, 'the enemy lost 784 suicide planes to score 216 hits on ships'.

'JUDY' KAMIKAZE TACTICS

Although the tactics behind flying an aircraft into a ship seemed straightforward enough once the pilot involved got past the psychological barrier of being killed in the resulting crash, as it turned out, throughout the kamikaze campaign the IJNAF constantly reassessed and refined its tactics in an effort to maximise success. The challenge was to get the pilot and his bomb-laden aircraft past Allied CAPs and anti-aircraft fire and into a position whereby he could crash into a moving, manoeuvring target.

In practice, it turned out that the challenge was more difficult than it initially appeared. The increasingly poorly trained IJNAF pilots found it more and more difficult to break through the massed ranks of fighters and intense anti-aircraft fire that they encountered as their adversaries woke up to the kamikaze threat. As a direct result of these factors, the tactics adopted by the IJNAF evolved considerably from when the kamikaze first appeared off Leyte to the last such operations on 15 August 1945 – the day that hostilities ended in the Pacific.

At the start of the campaign, the IJNAF typically used two different flight profiles when approaching the target. The first saw aircraft attack at low-level, closing on their targets at wavetop heights. This had the advantage of making it more difficult for ships' radar to detect the incoming aircraft, as well as increasing the risk of the vessel's defensive fire hitting friendly ships nearby (something that happened on occasion). This attack profile also made it more difficult for defending fighters to intercept kamikaze aircraft, even if they had been detected during their approach. Allied pilots attempting intercepts would have to divide their attention between shooting down their target aircraft and avoiding hitting the water while doing so.

This method of approach was possible during the first attacks that took place in late October 1944, for the naval aviators involved in these one-way missions were still relatively experienced and skilled. Indeed, they had completed the standard flying training courses, with some of the IJNAF pilots selected for early kamikaze operations in the Philippines even having combat experience under their belts. This method of attack was also used by the Formosa-based kamikaze units on occasion during the Battle of Okinawa, which commenced on 1 April 1945, underlining their reputation among their opponents that they were more skilled in suicide attacks than their Japan-based counterparts.

A pilot conducting a low-level attack needed to possess sufficient flying skills to maintain a consistently low altitude (30-50ft above the waves) on approach, and then be able to 'pop up' to 1300-1650 ft, before diving onto the target at an angle of 45 degrees or steeper. This approach could be combined with the use of nearby landmasses that created 'ground clutter' on ships' search radar screens to further cloak the attackers' presence. Such tactics were often used during kamikaze attacks on US Navy vessels sailing off Leyte and Luzon. Due to the pilot's need to maintain a visual reference with the target, the terminal dive following 'pop up' was sometimes done with the aircraft inverted. Such a manoeuvre required an even greater degree of skill.

The kamikaze pilots were also taught to approach their target from the stern whenever possible owing to the reduced concentration of anti-aircraft guns in the after part of the ship. In an attempt to counter this tactic, vessels under attack would turn so that their beams faced the oncoming aerial threat. While this presented a bigger target for the Japanese pilots to aim at, Allied navies judged that this was a risk worth taking as it allowed the crew to bring their full battery of anti-aircraft guns on one side of the ship into play.

The other flight profile attempted by kamikaze pilots, especially those flying the Suisei, was to attack from high-altitude. This entailed approaching the targeted ship at a ceiling of at least 20,000 ft, before losing height and picking up speed in a shallow 20-30-degree dive prior to finally entering a steeper 45-55-degree dive in the terminal phase of the attack. While simpler to execute, this approach still required a fair amount of skill.

In practice, although more damage could be done by an aircraft crashing into the target at a higher speed, it also made it harder for pilots to successfully hit a relatively small target turning at speed. When closing on a manoeuvring ship at speeds in excess of 400 mph, the pilot had little time available to make fine adjustments to his aim. Furthermore, his aircraft was less responsive to control inputs at higher speeds due to the airflow forces being exerted on its ailerons and rudder. That said, the D4Y was designed as a dive-bomber, so it was better suited to such attacks than more conventional types pressed into the kamikaze role.

Both profiles were tried in the Philippines, although by the time of the Battle of Okinawa the Japanese tended to approach mostly at low-to-medium altitudes ranging anywhere from 1500 ft up to 10,000 ft. Both wavetop and high altitude approaches were still very occasionally attempted, however, especially by Suisei-equipped units. The virtual abandonment of these original attack profiles was forced upon the Japanese when pilot quality deteriorated to a point where, for the most part, they were unable to effectively fly either.

The adoption of simpler attack profiles coincided with a dramatic increase in the number of aircraft being committed to kamikaze missions compared to the initial strikes. With the latter, only a solitary aircraft or a pair of attackers would target ships off Leyte. However, when low-to-medium altitude profiles were flown, ever larger formations of aircraft were being sent out against enemy ships to the point where waves of kamikazes were detected on Allied radar screens during the numbered Kikusui (Floating Chrysanthemum) operations off Okinawa. Such attacks were mounted in order to overwhelm the defenders, ensuring that at least some of the aircraft would 'leak' through the defences to achieve hits on Allied warships.

From the outset of the kamikaze campaign, it was determined that the aircraft tasked to carry out such attacks would need to carry explosive ordnance to improve the results of a successful crash into an enemy vessel. As the early strikes quickly demonstrated, an aircraft hitting even a relatively small warship such as a destroyer or destroyer escort did relatively little damage, given it was constructed much more lightly than the vessel it was crashing into. Indeed, only the aircraft's heavy engine block, in the right circumstances, could penetrate through steel hulls or decks. Nevertheless, this still was not enough to put a ship out of action or, on most occasions, significantly impair its fighting ability.

Therefore, kamikaze aircraft almost always carried explosive ordnance. Typically, this was a 551-lb bomb, of which the Japanese had several sub-types. The IJNAF called such a weapon of this weight class the No. 25 Model 1 Bomb. The Suisei, however, usually carried the less common 1102-lb teardrop-shaped armour-piercing weapon, which was known as the Type 2 No. 50 Model 1 Ordinary Bomb to the IJNAF.

OPERATIONS IN THE PHILIPPINES

As with most IJNAF units charged with defending the Philippines, the handful of Suisei-equipped air groups formed dedicated Special Attack flights manned by volunteer crews. The first of these was assigned to Dai-ichi Kamikaze Tokubetsu Kogekitai and flew its first mission on 25 October 1944. Subsequent Suisei-equipped Special Attack flights were assigned to Dai-Ni (i.e. 2nd) Kamikaze Tokubetsu Kogekitai and beyond, with the second Suisei special attack sorties taking place on 27 October.

The first recorded attack by Special Attack Suisei occurred on the morning of 25 October when escort carriers of TG 77.4 were targeted by A6M2s from 1st Kamikaze Special Attack Corps' Yamato-tai, the fighters being led from Cebu by a D4Y1 pathfinder/observer. A lone 'Judy' tokko from 1st Kamikaze Special Attack Corps' Suisei-tai also subsequently took off from Mabalacat, as did a handful of 'Zekes' (both tokko and escorts) from Shikishima-tai.

Having seen the 'Zekes' (from Shikishima-tai) strike a mortal blow to USS *St. Lo* (CVE-63) and badly damage USS *Kalinin Bay* (CVE-68) and USS *White Plains* (CVE-66), the 'Judy' pilot (probably from Cebu) made a run on USS *Kitkun Bay* (CVE-71), which had previously been struck a glancing blow by one of the A6M2s. The carrier's anti-aircraft batteries scored several hits on the diving Suisei, causing it to burst into flames and break up just prior to falling into the sea close to the ship. Several fragments hit the vessel, including the aircraft's horizontal stabiliser assembly which came to rest on the flightdeck.

The attack by the D4Y1 signalled the end of the first engagement between dedicated kamikaze aircraft and their enemy, with the damage inflicted on the US Navy by this new tactic totalling one escort carrier sunk and four damaged to varying degrees. While a seemingly modest haul, this still represented a significant proportion of the losses suffered by the US Navy during the Battle of Leyte Gulf. The results of 25 October would have also assured Vice Admiral Onishi and other proponents of the kamikaze that their decision to adopt such tactics had been more than justified.

On 29 October, 18 aircraft ('Zekes', 'Vals' and 'Judys') from seven kamikaze units took off from Nichols Field, south of Manila, and targeted Rear Admiral Gerald F Bogan's TG 38.2, comprised of the carriers *Intrepid*, *Hancock*, *Bunker Hill*, *Cabot* and USS *Independence* (CVL-22), off Luzon. A solitary D3A struck *Intrepid*, with the remaining aircraft being shot down – two 'Judys' were claimed by VF-7 (embarked in *Hancock*) and two fell to VF-18 (embarked in *Intrepid*).

The escort carriers of TG 77.4 were targeted by multiple A6M2s and two D4Y1s on 25 October 1944 during the first recorded attack by Special Attack Suisei. *Kitkun Bay* was more fortunate than its sister-ship *St. Lo*, with the former only being struck a glancing blow by a 'Zeke' in the attack that sunk the latter vessel. A short while later, a 'Judy' (almost certainly the pathfinder/observer aircraft for 1st Kamikaze Special Attack Corps' Yamato-tai) made a run on *Kitkun Bay* from astern, although the carrier's anti-aircraft batteries scored several hits on the diving bomber. The D4Y1 burst into flames, as seen here, and broke up just prior to falling into the sea close to the ship (*NARA*)

The strikes against Luzon by the fast carrier groups started to develop a pattern during the month of November, with one or two carrier task groups hitting targets on the island every five days or so following replenishments at sea or brief visits to the Pacific Fleet's anchorage at Ulithi Atoll, in the Caroline Islands. The tokko-tai units usually responded to these strikes, although without success until 25 November when TGs 38.2 and 38.3 arrived off Leyte prior to their air groups again taking the fight to the enemy.

Kamikaze aircraft attacked TG 38.2 from just after noon, with A6M5s hitting *Intrepid* and *Cabot*. It was TG 38.3's turn to be targeted at 1255 hrs, when two aircraft appeared off *Essex*'s starboard quarter just as the carrier was in the midst of launching its air group on a strike mission. Both were immediately fired upon by the carrier's anti-aircraft batteries until they disappeared into a nearby cloud bank, only to reappear, separately, minutes later in their attack dives.

Although the lead tokko had its left wing set alight (as seen in a series of spectacular photographs taken from on board the ship as the aeroplane inexorably closed on its target), the pilot succeeded in hitting *Essex* on its port side amidships and the aircraft exploded in a fireball. Fifteen crewmen were killed and 44 wounded, most of them manning a number of 20 mm guns that were destroyed on the port side of the ship. The explosion inevitably started a fire, although this was quickly doused before it could cause any structural damage. The second aircraft had crashed harmlessly into the sea 800 yards away after it was repeatedly struck by anti-aircraft fire.

Essex's crew identified their attackers as B6N 'Jill' or B7A 'Grace' torpedo-bombers, although the previously mentioned photographs of the lead aircraft plunging into the ship from astern show it clearly to be a late model D4Y3 dive-bomber bearing the number '17' on its tail. Identifying the aircraft that undertook this attack is thus a relatively straightforward task, given there was just a single kamikaze unit that launched 'Judys' that day. This was 4th Kamikaze Special Attack Unit's Katori-tai (drawn from 3rd Attack Hikotai of 701st Kokutai), which sortied two aircraft from Mabalacat at 1130 hrs. The lead D4Y3 was flown by Lt(jg) Tadashi Tanabe (pilot) and Ens Taro Kudo (observer), while FPO1cs Yoshinori Yamaguchi

Still wearing his steel helmet, a gunner manning one of the deck edge 20 mm Oerlikon guns on board *Kitkun Bay* stares intently at the severed tail section of the 'Judy' that he and his shipmates had just shot down (*NARA*)

This photograph was taken by a combat cameraman on board *Ticonderoga*, which was sailing to the port side of *Essex* when the carrier came under attack by the D4Y3s of Lt(jg) Tadashi Tanabe and Ens Taro Kudo and CPOs Yoshinori Yamaguchi (pilot) and Masa Sakaki (observer) from 4th Kamikaze Special Attack Unit's Katori-tai on 25 November 1944. This still image taken from the motion picture footage clearly shows numerous aircraft spotted on the after part of CV-9's flightdeck that were missed by the 'Judy'. Had they been hit, the damage inflicted on the carrier would almost certainly have been far worse, as these machines were both fuelled and armed (*NARA*)

A billowing cloud of smoke and flame mark the spot where the D4Y3 struck *Essex*. Note the plumes of spray ahead of the carrier where parts of the aircraft had hit the water following its impact with the ship. One of these was almost certainly caused by the 'Judy's' single bomb, which was flung overboard without exploding. The ship's action report suggested that the lack of serious damage inflicted on CV-9 was due to the 'Judy' being unarmed. However, IJNAF records indicate that both aircraft were indeed carrying a single 1102-lb Type 2 No. 50 Model 1 Ordinary Bomb each (*NARA*)

(pilot) and Tadashi Sakaki (observer) were in the second aircraft. They had been tasked with attacking an enemy carrier task group approximately 150 nautical miles east-southeast of Mabalacat.

Several sources attribute the hit on *Essex* to Yamaguchi. However, given that the ship's crew reported the carrier being struck by the lead aircraft, it would seem that it was Lt(jg) Tanabe's 'Judy' that exploded upon crashing into the port side of the vessel.

Aside from the still photographs taken from on board *Essex*, this attack was also immortalised on film by a combat cameraman shooting from nearby USS *Ticonderoga* (CV-14). His motion picture footage shows numerous aircraft spotted on the after part of *Essex*'s flightdeck, which were missed by the 'Judy'. Had they been hit, the damage inflicted on the carrier would invariably have been far worse. The ship's action report suggested that the lack of serious damage caused by the D4Y3 was due to it not carrying a bomb. However, IJNAF records indicate that both aircraft were armed with a single 1102-lb Type 2 No. 50 Model 1 Ordinary Bomb each. Given that the D4Y3 hit very near the port edge of the flightdeck, the bomb itself was clearly flung overboard without exploding.

Two days later, several Suisei (from 5th Hikotai, assigned to 634th Kokutai, and 3rd Hikotai, assigned to 701st Kokutai) were involved in a general all-out attack on US forces that were fighting in the city of Tacloban, on Leyte. Furthermore, Japanese records note that the nine kamikaze and 26 other aircraft that had been sent into action that day had failed to carry out their planned attacks due to poor weather over Tacloban and the intervention of enemy fighters.

The next recorded action involving a Suisei took place on 7 December, when the kamikaze units enjoyed their most successful day of the Philippine campaign in terms of vessels sunk – a destroyer, a high-speed transport and a landing ship (medium) were all lost. They were all supporting landings south of Ormoc City, on Leyte's west coast, by the US Army's 77th Infantry Division. A fourth ship, the destroyer USS *Lamson* (DD-367), was badly damaged according to the vessel's action report;

'A Tony came around from behind Himuquitan Island and made a low, fast approach on our starboard quarter. Control managed to get on the plane at about a range of 1000 yards, but guns Nos. 1 and 2 were in the blind [masked by the ship's superstructure]. The plane came in weaving and strafing. Its approach was on our starboard quarter 30 ft off the water, but it crossed slightly to amidships as we went hard left. It hit No. 2 stack with its right wing and spun around, crashing into the after port corner of the transmitter room, and drove on in until the propeller was imbedded on the outside of the after Control bulkhead.'

The hit, and subsequent fire, killed 21 of the ship's crew and almost resulted in *Lamson* being abandoned and sunk, with Capt William M Cole, commander of Destroyer Squadron 5, deciding that preparations should be made to sink it. However, firefighting efforts proved to be successful, and the vessel was subsequently towed to safety.

A number of accounts detailing the *Lamson* attack agree with the ship's action report that its attacker was a Ki-61, with others identifying it only as a 'single-engined fighter'. IJAAF records indicate that no 'Tonys' – readily identifiable by their inline engines, which were rarely used by Japanese aircraft – undertook kamikaze attacks on 7 December, or indeed at any point during the entire campaign in the Philippines. Therefore, it is almost certain that *Lamson*'s attacker was a D4Y1/2. There were several IJNAF kamikaze units in action that day, with a single 'Judy' from Chihaya-tai (accompanied by four 'Zeke' escorts) taking off from Mabalacat soon after midday.

There were a few more kamikaze attacks off Leyte in the following days, but by this time the Japanese high command had realised the island was lost. Concurrently, the Americans started preparing for the invasion of Mindoro Island, codenamed Operation *Love III*. With the newly captured airfields on Leyte too far from Luzon, and specifically Manila, to allow land-based USAAF aircraft to support the invasion of this key island in the Philippines, Mindoro was deemed to be the logical choice for the next amphibious assault thanks to its coastal plains and minimal Japanese presence. An area near the town of San Jose at the southwestern tip of the island was chosen as the spot for the initial landings, scheduled for 15 December.

The seaborne invasion forces were located by Japanese reconnaissance aircraft a full two days before the planned landings as they traversed the Bohol Sea and entered the Sulu Sea between the islands of Mindanao and Negros. Despite IJNAF air power in-theatre now being on the wane, a kamikaze strike force was hastily assembled at Mabalacat. Of the 26 aircraft brought together for an attack on 14 December, three of them were D4Ys from 3rd Hikotai. One of the Suisei was crewed by PO2c Takeji Takebe (pilot) and group leader Lt Yonosuke Iguchi (observer), who had flown with WO Shinsaku Yamakawa in the attack described in the previous chapter.

Inclement weather caused the majority of the kamikaze to call off the mission, although Iguchi's aircraft pressed on. His final radio transmission came through at 1237 hrs, when he reported that his pilot had commenced a dive on enemy warships. The US Navy reported no damage being inflicted on any of its vessels that day.

Kamikaze units would enjoy more success on the morning of 15 December as the invasion of Mindoro began. With the fleet mostly sitting off San Jose, both the IJNAF and IJAAF despatched whatever air power they could muster – five groups of aircraft were sent aloft, four of them from the IJNAF. Only three of the groups were sent against the invasion fleet, however. It was the 9th Kongo-tai force, led by Lt Susumu Aoki and consisting of 12 'Zekes' and a solitary 'Judy', from Mabalacat that was almost certainly responsible for the damage inflicted on the escort carrier USS *Marcus Island* (CVE-77) and the destroyers USS *Howorth* (DD-592) and USS *Paul Hamilton* (DD-590), and the sinking of *LST-472* and *LST-738*.

By year-end, the number of serviceable Suisei in the Philippines had plummeted, and few attrition replacements were now reaching units from Formosa.

6 January 1945 turned out to be the climax of the kamikaze offensive off Luzon, with Japanese records indicating a total of 44 aircraft (38 IJNAF and six IJAAF) being sent against the invasion fleet as vessels arrived in the Lingayen Gulf. Starting before noon and continuing throughout the day, the IJNAF sortied 35 'Zekes', with two 'Judys' from Kyokujitsu-tai and a single 'Jill' from Hachiman-tai rounding out the service's contribution that day.

The attackers hit in roughly three separate waves – the first just before noon, the second at around 1430 hrs and the third from 1730 hrs onward. A total of 15 ships were struck, with the high-speed destroyer minesweeper USS *Long* (DMS-12) being sunk after completing its first sweep of Lingayen Gulf. Amongst those damaged was the heavy cruiser USS *Louisville* (CA-28), which had also been one of 13 ships hit the previous day when the US Navy's entry into Lingayen Gulf prompted an intense Japanese reaction.

Louisville's crew reported being attacked by a 'Kate' and a 'Val' at 1730 hrs, with the former crashing into its starboard signal bridge – 41 sailors were killed and 125 wounded. A piece of wreckage that appears to have been an inner landing gear door was recovered by crewman John Duffy. It was adorned with kanji stencilling that, when translated, read 'Suisei Model 11, Aichi 156x' (last number unclear). This means the vessel was actually struck by a D4Y1, making it likely that the attacker was the Kyokujitsu-tai aircraft that had taken off from Mabalacat crewed by Lt(jg) Tadashi Fukino and Ens Seisaku Miyake.

Despite having been extensively damaged by two kamikaze hits in 24 hours, and with no functioning bridge, *Louisville* shelled the invasion beaches and shot down several enemy aircraft over the next 72 hours, before withdrawing on 9 January and proceeding to Mare Island Navy Yard, north of San Francisco, for repairs. The heavy cruiser would return to the action off Okinawa in late April.

There is no further mention by either side of 'Judys' being involved in kamikaze attacks through to 13 January, when Japanese aircraft flew their last successful suicide missions during this campaign. IJNAF and IJAAF air power in-theatre had by then been almost utterly destroyed. However, the end of kamikaze operations in the Philippines only saw the threat materialising elsewhere. In fact, the use of suicide tactics amplified as the Japanese grew increasingly desperate in their attempts to halt the Allied advance on the Home Islands.

OTHER THEATRES

As the Americans established themselves on Luzon during the course of January 1945 and Japanese air activity over the Philippines dwindled into insignificance, TF 38 aircraft continued to conduct strikes against enemy-occupied territory in order to prevent the remaining forces on the island from being reinforced. On 12 January the fast carriers struck Indochina, before turning their attention on Formosa, Hong Kong, Hainan and Canton on the 15th and 16th. After a break to refuel, they attacked targets on Formosa once again on the 20th and 21st and Okinawa on the 22nd, before heading back to Ulithi Atoll to prepare for the invasion of Iwo Jima.

The IJNAF responded to these raids predominantly with conventional attacks, although on 21 January three separate tokko-tai sortied in search of the enemy. The first two flights to depart Tainan, on the southwest coast of Formosa, consisted of 'Zekes', whose pilots had been instructed to search for enemy ships spotted 80 nautical miles southeast of Taitung, on Formosa's east coast. The A6M5s were followed aloft by five 'Judys' from 2nd Niitaka-tai, also based at Tainan. Led by Lt(jg) Kozo Nishida, the dive-bombers took off between 1130 hrs and 1150 hrs and were vectored towards another task force reported to be sailing 50 nautical miles east-southeast of Taitung.

Two 'Zekes' from 1st Koku Kantai Reisen-tai and the five 'Judys' subsequently attacked ships from TG 38.3 shortly after noon. The fast carrier *Ticonderoga* and the light carrier USS *Langley* (CVL-27) were both hit (the latter by a bomb and the former by two kamikazes) as the pair steamed 100 nautical miles to the east of Taitung. *Langley* and nearby *Essex*, which had closed with the carriers following the sighting of enemy aircraft, reported that the vessels were attacked by 'Judys'. Two were shot down, with the third Suisei being the second of two kamikaze aircraft to hit *Ticonderoga* – no fewer than 143 sailors perished in these two attacks, with a further 202 being wounded.

TG 38.3's stated location tallies closely with that given to the 'Zekes' of 1st Koku Kantai Reisen-tai, and it is highly likely they were responsible for the initial attack, with the D4Ys of 2nd Niitaka-tai following close behind.

After a period of rest and refit at Ulithi Atoll in the wake of the Formosa strikes in January, TF 38 became TF 58 again, with the change in command seeing the fleet transferred from Third Fleet back to Fifth Fleet control as the US Navy prepared for the invasion of Iwo Jima. Part of the Volcano Islands group approximately halfway between the Mariana Islands and Japan's Home Islands, Iwo Jima had been increasingly reinforced since early 1944. This took on an added urgency following the loss of the Marianas in mid-1944 and the invasion of the Philippines in October.

The assault on Iwo Jima commenced on 19 February. Despite the presence of two airfields on the islands, and the partial completion of a third, there were no Japanese aircraft on Iwo Jima to oppose the operation. Instead, on the 18th, as the invasion fleet started to arrive offshore, preparations were made to send a kamikaze task force from Japan against the Allied warships. This mission fell to 601st Kokutai at Katori, east of Tokyo, which scraped together a mixed force of 32 aircraft under the overall command of Lt Hiroshi Murakawa. Known as 2nd Mitate-tai, the unit was comprised of 12 D4Y3s from 1st Attack Hikotai, an identical number of A6M5s from 310th Fighter Hikotai and eight B6N2s from 254th Attack Hikotai. Facing this understrength force was an invasion fleet numbering more than 450 ships.

2nd Mitate-tai's D4Ys and B6Ns were divided between five units known as Kogekitai (Attack Units), with three of them made up of four 'Judys'

A rare photograph of a single-seat D4Y4 of 601st Kokutai's 3rd Attack Hikotai being serviced at Koromo, in Aichi Prefecture, in the late spring of 1945. Just 296 examples of the kamikaze-optimised Suisei Special Attack Bomber Model 43 were built by Aichi between February and August 1945 (*PD-Japan-oldphoto*)

armed with a 1102-lb Type 2 No. 50 Model 1 Ordinary Bomb each. They were escorted by four 'Zekes'. The remaining two Kogekitai had four 'Jills' each.

The original plan was to attack the invasion force on 20 February, but bad weather pushed this back a day to the 21st. With Iwo Jima more than 650 nautical miles away, 2nd Mitate-tai had to refuel en route at Hachijo-jima, 175 nautical miles to the south of Katori. Once this had been successfully accomplished, the 'Judys' took off from Hachijo-jima at 1400 hrs and the 'Jills' followed two hours later, their crews intending to time their attacks for the late afternoon and early evening. Technical issues started bedevilling 2nd Mitate-tai at this point, with various aircraft being forced to drop out. All the 'Judys' pressed on, however.

The D4Y3s and their A6M5 escorts were detected by the fleet just before 1630 hrs as the aircraft approached on a grey, overcast afternoon. The tokko crews quickly singled out the veteran carrier USS *Saratoga* (CV-3), the ship having been detached from TG 58.5 that morning with a screening force of just three destroyers and sent to the northeast of Iwo Jima to provide night CAP over the island and undertake nocturnal 'heckler' missions over Chichi-jima. The carrier was detected before it had reached its assigned station, with the six aircraft of 2nd Kogekitai starting their attacks at 1700 hrs.

The ship's crew correctly identified their opponents as a mix of 'Zekes' and 'Judys', and four of them – along with two or three bombs – hit *Saratoga* in just a matter of minutes. The carrier's forward flightdeck was badly holed, leaving it temporarily incapable of flight operations, and the hangar bay was also badly damaged.

More kamikazes targeted the invasion fleet off Iwo Jima at 1720 hrs, with the 6250-ton net-laying ship USS *Keokuk* (AKN-4), *LST-477* and *LST-809* being attacked in quick succession as they steamed with similar vessels to the southeast of Iwo Jima. *Keokuk*'s crew identified the aircraft that approached from almost dead ahead as a 'Jill', and despite it being set on fire, the kamikaze clipped the vessel's No. 1 20 mm gun mount and forward searchlight, and disintegrated as it tore through the ship's starboard side and midships gig davit. Its bomb (estimated to be a 551-lb weapon) exploded on *Keokuk*'s main deck to starboard moments later. The aircraft and its detonating ordnance destroyed the ship's entire starboard gun battery, save for a single 20 mm weapon, and started fires on board, although they had been extinguished by 1850 hrs. Seventeen sailors were either killed or listed as missing, with 44 wounded. Prior to being struck, the ship's gunners had been credited with shooting down one of the four aircraft sighted approaching the group.

2nd Kogekitai reported encountering an enemy transport convoy at 1620 hrs, and it is likely that it was this unit that attacked the LSTs and *Keokuk*. Sailors from the latter ship recovered two bodies from the wreckage of their attacker, which would suggest that it was a two-seat 'Judy' and not a three-seat 'Jill' that struck the vessel. The longer fuselage length of the Suisei could make its wingspan appear shorter, and this may be why the two LSTs misidentified their attackers as clipped-wing 'Hamps'.

The remaining aircraft of 3rd Kogekitai never reached their targets, as they were intercepted by US Navy Hellcats near Chichi-jima. Two 'Judys' and two 'Zekes' subsequently force-landed there due to battle damage. A solitary 'Judy' and three 'Zekes' that had taken off later from Hachijo-jima also ran into American fighters near Iwo Jima, with the D4Y being shot down and an A6M crashing as it attempted to land at Chichi-jima. These were almost certainly the aircraft intercepted by Hellcats from VF-53 embarked in *Saratoga*, the fighter pilots claiming three aircraft shot down and a fourth as a probable.

The attacks on 21 February were the only serious attempts made by Japanese aircraft to disrupt the landings at Iwo Jiima. As a postscript to these missions, on 1 March a single 'Judy' (flown by Chief Flyer Nao Kawasaki and FPO Yoshio Kobayashi, who had failed to complete their mission eight days earlier) from 2nd Mitate-tai left Chichi-jima intent on targeting shipping off Iwo Jima. No results were obtained.

As the planned invasion of Okinawa (codenamed Operation *Iceberg*), scheduled for 1 April 1945, rapidly approached, TF 58's final task prior to the launching of the campaign was to strike the numerous airfields on Kyushu – the southwesternmost of Japan's three main islands. The US Navy knew full well that both the IJNAF and the IJAAF would mount their principal aerial response (including kamikazes) to the amphibious landings from these bases.

On 18 March, four days of operations against Kyushu, and beyond, commenced, during which time carrier-based fighter pilots claimed almost 300 Japanese aircraft shot down (including five 'Judys'). Many more were destroyed on the ground as their airfields were repeatedly attacked, effectively curtailing Japanese aerial activity in the two weeks leading up to the invasion of Okinawa.

The Japanese had tracked TF 58's progress as it headed toward Kyushu, and initially they were unsure if the US Navy was carrying out a carrier-based sweep of the area or launching an actual invasion. As it became clear that it was in fact the former, the IJNAF and IJAAF opted to limit their aerial counterattacks in order to save the bulk of their remaining aircraft for another day. Nevertheless, a handful of both conventional attacks and kamikaze missions were generated, although the modest number of aircraft involved meant that the Japanese enjoyed only a limited return for their effort.

A kamikaze strike force consisting of 50 aircraft had targeted TF 58 on 18 March, inflicting light damage on the carriers USS *Enterprise* (CV-6) and USS *Franklin* (CV-13). D4Y3s from 103rd and 105th Attack Hikotais of 701st Kokutai, comprising Kamikaze Tokubetsu Kogekitai Kikusui Butai Suisei-tai, had participated in this operation.

The most significant success enjoyed by the IJNAF off Kyushu came on the 19th, when around 20 Suisei targeted TF 58. One of the Suisei singled out *Franklin*, whose Carrier Air Group 5 was just about to launch an early morning strike mission against Kure naval base. The lone D4Y3 performed a conventional dive-bombing run that saw the aircraft hit the carrier with two 551-lb bombs that pierced the flightdeck and exploded in the hangar bay, setting off additional explosions and raging fires. The 'Judy' then attempted to make good its escape. The calamity of this attack was captured in an article written by David H Lippman for *World War II* magazine;

'*Franklin*'s Combat Information Center (CIC) reported at 0706 hrs, "Bogey orbiting on port beam, range about 12 miles". Firing Director One picked up a moving target bearing ten degrees, but then lost it in the clutter of TF 58 launching her planes.

'At 0707 hrs, the ship's navigator, Cdr Stephen Jurika, saw an enemy plane sweep over his head. It was a Japanese Yokosuka D4Y Judy dive-bomber, and it dropped two 551-lb bombs on *Franklin*. The twin blasts hurled Jurika into the air, and he hit the steel overhead.

'The first bomb ripped through 3-inch armor to the hangar deck. The second bomb detonated two decks below that, near the chief petty officers' quarters. The explosions knocked the ship's commanding officer, Capt Leslie E Gehres, off his feet. He saw great sheets of flame envelope the flightdeck, the anti-aircraft batteries and catwalks. The forward elevator – weighing 32 tons – rose in the air and then disappeared in a great column of flame and black smoke.

'Five bombers, 14 torpedo-bombers and 12 fighters were on the flight and hangar decks, carrying 36,000 gallons of gas and 30 tons of bombs and rockets between them. They became an inferno.

'*Franklin* was listing at 13 degrees. Her radar was out, her CIC and communications gone. Gehres thought his ship was damaged on the starboard side and turned *Franklin* in that direction to put the wind on the port bow. That move instead fanned flames near the fuelled aircraft. *Franklin* presented a terrifying sight to the rest of TF 58. On a battleship 1000 yards off, crewmen stared in horror at the carrier covered in smoke and flame. Marine Corporal Bill Clinger saw the Judy that had bombed *Franklin* whiz over his head. Lt Scotty Campbell saw *Franklin*'s bombs and rockets exploding in all directions.

'One observer reacted immediately to the situation. A Corsair orbiting *Franklin* swooped on the Judy and shot it down.

'On the bridge, Cdr Jurika suggested to Capt Gehres that he turn *Franklin* into the wind. He steered the carrier onto course 355, due north, which put relative wind on the starboard bow and allowed firefighters to work fore to aft. It also put *Franklin* on a 24-knot course directly toward Japan. But there was no time to think about that. A three-inch gasoline line aft had ruptured. Bombs, rockets and 0.50-cal ammunition were still exploding. Then a 40 mm ready-service magazine exploded. This new blast lifted *Franklin* and spun her to starboard. A sheet of flame rose 400 ft over the carrier, rupturing the flightdeck in a dozen places.

'More carnage and chaos soon erupted on the scene. Aircraft engines flew up in the air. Tremendous explosions rocked the ship. Aircraft and ship parts rained down on survivors. A 100-ft high wall of fire rose over the island while aircraft ordnance and ammunition for both aircraft and the ship exploded. A great smoke plume ascended above the clouds. Tiny Tim rockets carried by the ship's aircraft continued to shoot off all over. *Franklin's* sailors, however, were determined to save the ship and grabbed hoses to put out the flames.'

Franklin lost steering control at 0911 hrs, and by 1000 hrs it lay still in the water and listing to one side. The heavy cruiser USS *Pittsburgh* (CA-72) signalled at 1128 hrs that it could take the vessel under tow, by which point the fires on board *Franklin* were now almost under control.

At 1254 hrs, the carrier was again attacked by a 'Judy'. While the aircraft managed to drop a large bomb, it missed its mark and exploded in the water 200 yards from *Franklin*. Anti-aircraft fire from the carrier then downed the dive-bomber. In the early afternoon *Pittsburgh* took *Franklin* under tow at three knots, the carrier initially being taken to Ulithi prior to being sent home to New York for major repairs. It would be out of commission for the rest of the war. More than 800 sailors and Marines aboard the vessel perished in the attack, with a further 487 being wounded.

Sister-ship USS *Wasp* (CV-18) was also hit by a 551-lb bomb that morning, the weapon reportedly being dropped by another 'Judy'. The bomb punched a hole in the flightdeck and the armour-plated hangar deck, before finally exploding in the crew's galley. Many sailors were having breakfast at the time, having been at general quarters all night preparing aircraft for a dawn attack on Kyushu. The explosion killed 102 crew.

The deadly attacks on TF 58 between 18 and 21 March had been undertaken by D4Y3s of the Kikusui Butai, which was the name given to the kamikaze task force initially created from Kyushu-based IJNAF Kokutais (and led by Vice Admiral Matome Ugaki) in early 1945. With the strikes on Kyushu, more tokko-tai were rapidly formed under the control of the Kikusui Butai, starting with Suisei-tai that drew on men and machines from 701st Kokutai.

Aside from *Franklin* and *Wasp*, the destroyer USS *Halsey Powell* (DD-686) also suffered terrible damage at the hands of Suisei-tai. At 1454 hrs on 20 March, while sailing alongside the carrier *Hancock* in order to receive fuel and transfer mail and personnel, an enemy aircraft was reported in the vicinity. As the destroyer hastily cast off the starboard side of the carrier, the latter opened fire when gunners spotted the Japanese aircraft approaching in a steep dive from the port side. Hits on the tokko caused it to disintegrate as the aircraft passed over the carrier. However, a significant chunk of the airframe struck the destroyer's fantail and one of its wings

TF 58 mounted a four-day offensive against airfields on Kyushu from 18 March 1945, during which time the IJNAF and IJAAF opted to limit their aerial counterattacks in order to save the bulk of their remaining aircraft for another day once it became clear that the attacks were not the precursor to invasion. The greatest success achieved by the IJNAF by some margin in response to these attacks was the bombing of *Franklin* on 19 March by a lone D4Y3 from Kikusui Butai, the aircraft hitting the carrier with two 551-lb bombs – it was not a tokko attack, however, as the 'Judy' crew did not crash into the vessel. The bombs caused a raging fire to break out on board that killed 807 crew and wounded 487 (*NARA*)

clipped the after 5-in gun. A fire was started by the impact, which also caused flooding and jammed the rudder at 15 degrees to port.

After nearly being run over by *Hancock* as the destroyer strayed across the carrier's bow, *Halsey Powell* came to a stop so that its crew could assess the damage. Having temporarily left the task group's protective screen, the vessel relied on the assistance of other destroyers to help effect emergency repairs. DD-686 subsequently re-joined TF 58 once it was found that the crew could steer the ship by varying engine speeds. Despite considerable damage being caused to the destroyer, casualties were relatively light – nine killed and 30 wounded.

Halsey Powell's crew identified the attacker as a 'Zeke', although it was almost certainly a 'Judy' from Suisei-tai. Seven D4Ys from 701st Kokutai had taken off on kamikaze missions that day, with three from 103rd Hikotai departing from Kokubu No. 1 airfield between 1250 hrs and 1356 hrs and four more (one from 5th and three from 105th Hikotai) being despatched from Kokubu No. 2 airfield between 1424 hrs and 1505 hrs. Their crews were tasked with engaging a carrier task force east of Kyushu. Given the timing of the attack, it was probably an aircraft from the former group that targeted *Hancock* but hit *Halsey Powell* instead.

On 22 March TF 58 headed south for a series of strikes against Okinawa and the Ryukyu Islands ahead of the forthcoming invasion. The carriers returned to attack Kyushu on 28–29 March, although by then US forces had already landed on some of Okinawa's outlying islands. Both the IJNAF and the IJAAF again refused to engage TF 58 on any significant scale, with the only kamikazes sent against the carriers being a pair of 'Judys' from 2nd Suisei-tai on the afternoon of the 29th. One of these narrowly missed USS *Yorktown* (CV-10) off Tanegashima, disintegrating from the combined fire of the ship's guns and a pair of pursuing Hellcats from *Langley*.

OKINAWA

With the Philippines effectively liberated by late February 1945 and US forces having landed on Iwo Jima on the 19th of that same month, Allied attention now turned to Okinawa – the largest and most developed of the Ryukyu chain of islands. If it could be taken, Okinawa would provide the Allies with a key staging area and strategically critical launchpad for the invasion of the Japanese mainland. Located approximately 350 nautical miles south of Kyushu, the island was within range of most IJAAF and IJNAF aircraft based in southern Japan. Units on Formosa had an even shorter distance to fly in order to reach the waters off Okinawa, which Vice Admiral Matome Ugaki had decided would be the next battleground for his kamikazes.

In an effort to improve the effectiveness of their air operations (which included tokko attacks) following the failed defence of the Philippines, the IJAAF and IJNAF made an attempt to unify their command structure with the creation of 6th Koku gun (Air Army) in early 1945. An agreement was also reached on the targets each service would concentrate on, as laid out in the Joint Central Agreement on Air Operations issued in March 1945 as part of the IJNAF's Directive No. 540. Known as the *Ten-Go* Operation Plan, it called for units from both services to deploy to the East China Sea area in the defence of the Ryukyu Islands. Once here, the less-capable pilots of the IJAAF would concentrate on attacking transport convoys and their escorts, while the IJNAF would target enemy carrier striking task forces and other warships with both kamikaze attacks and conventional torpedo- and dive-bomber operations.

Undermining these grand plans for cooperation was the poor quality of the aircrew, and the training they had received, by this late stage in the war. Indeed, the number of combat-ready naval aviators had declined from the heady days at the start of the wider Pacific War to the point where the IJNAF stated in January 1945 that it did not expect its aircraft and crew strength to be ready for battle until May at the earliest. This decision, however, was taken out of the IJNAF's hands with the invasion of Okinawa, which commenced with the occupation of Kerama Retto – a small group of islands 17 nautical miles southwest of Okinawa.

FP01c Yoshiji Takeda and FP02c Shigeki Yamaguchi of 252nd Kokutai pose in front of their D4Y3 just before departing Katori for Kokubu on 31 March 1945 prior to the start of the Okinawa campaign. Above the aircraft's tail number is the 'Z' Flag, the trademark of 3rd Attack Hikotai at this time. The weather that day was unsettled, and two Suisei crashed near Kanbara, in Shizuoka Prefecture, killing four airmen, including FP01c Takeda and FP02c Yamaguchi. Three more D4Y3s from 3rd Attack Hikotai were also lost in crash landings (*Tony Holmes Collection*)

Following the 18–22 March strikes on Kyushu, TF 58 arrived off Okinawa to 'soften up' Japanese positions prior to the actual landings, scheduled for 26 March at Kerama Retto and 1 April on Okinawa proper. The presence of hundreds of carrier-based fighters in the area meant the tokko-tai were unable to muster more than token resistance in the days immediately leading up to the invasion of Kerama Retto, much less achieve any successes.

The only action involving 'Judys' off Okinawa immediately prior to the commencement of Operation *Iceberg* occurred at 0600 hrs on 27 March when ten D4Y3s from Kyushu-based 2nd Suisei-tai, staging via Kikaijima Island in the Amami archipelago, attempted to attack TF 58's carriers off Okinawa. They met with no success.

When American troops began landing on Okinawa on the morning of 1 April, Japanese forces were not ready to initiate the *Ten-Go* Operation Plan, despite Combined Fleet issuing an alert a week earlier. The IJNAF's Fifth Air Fleet in Kyushu (charged with overseeing all IJNAF and IJAAF operations in *Ten-Go*) was still recovering from the losses it had suffered the previous month. Third Air Fleet (flying from airfields in the Kanto Plain in the defence of Honshu) and Sixth Air Army, which had 25 Special Attack units to deploy, were still moving their units to Kyushu. Finally, many of the Special Attack tokko-tai controlled by Tenth Air Fleet (activated on 1 March 1945 to take over command of new operational units converted from training groups) were still undergoing training.

With the invasion confirmed through reconnaissance flights, Tenth Air Fleet was, nevertheless, ordered by the IJNAF to move its units to Kanoya, in the southeastern region of Kyushu. The movement of aircraft and personnel took time, so a massed attack on the American invasion fleet had to be delayed. In the interim, both the IJAAF and IJNAF mounted daily reconnaissance flights to find and track the Allied carriers in order to initiate attacks on the invasion force with conventional aircraft and a small number of kamikazes.

Ens Yoshimasa Takimoto and Ens Tamotsu Yokoyama with D4Y2-S 'YoD-238'. Both were assigned to 302nd Kokutai's land reconnaissance unit prior to transferring to 2nd Hikotai. Takimoto and Yokoyama were killed in action on 12 April 1945 in a tokko attack whilst serving with Hyakurigahara Kokutai (*Tony Holmes Collection*)

The evolution of the D4Y into a nightfighter and the aerial combat successes credited to the Yokosuka Night Fighter Unit were described in 1975 by Lt Shiro Kurotori;

'The Night Fighter Unit I was assigned to in 1944 was unique amongst the many day fighter squadrons equipped with the Zero-sen. Its formation was overseen by Atsugi base commander, Cdr Yasuna Kozono, who suggested the fitment of 20 mm sloping guns into the Suisei. Aside from its officer cadre, the unit was manned by superior non-commissioned officers.

'The sloping cannon-armed Suisei was the aircraft Cdr Kozono anticipated the most, and the first one was destroyed after Lt Yamada crash-landed following a successful combat mission on 24–25 May.

'The Yokosuka Night Fighter Unit conducted a lot of research in a short period of time on several modified variants of frontline aircraft types, undertaking test flights during daylight hours and then being assigned to the defence of Tokyo at night. It was not unusual for crews to fly six times a day, followed by one or two operational sorties at night.'

One of the most successful IJNAF nightfighter units of the Pacific War, 302nd Kokutai served as the 'Imperial Capital's Air Defence Battle Unit'. Established at Kisarazu on 1 March 1944 and transferred to Atsugi later that same month, the air group was initially intended to have been equipped with 48 day fighters and 24 nightfighters. By November, it was composed of 1st Hikotai (ten J2M Raidens and 27 A6M5 Zero-sens), 2nd Hikotai (six D4Y2-S) and 3rd Hikotai (15 J1N1-S Gekkos and two P1Y1-S Gingas).

2nd Kokutai had to make do with only a limited number of Suisei throughout its brief existence, its force consisting of just eight aircraft

Posing atop the observer's seat of his D4Y1-C, FPO1c Ryo-ichi Yamamoto of 302nd Kokutai later transferred to the air group's Night Fighter Unit upon its formation (*Tony Holmes Collection*)

(three of which were usually operational) by 1 June 1944. The number of D4Y2-Ss had grown to ten by 1 October (with six operational) and 20 (but again with only six operational) by 1 November. Its operational strength stood at nine Suisei on 1 January 1945, 15 on 1 March and 27 on 1 May.

Such modest numbers meant that 2nd Hikotai only enjoyed limited success in the air defence role following its operational debut during the night of 24–25 November 1944, with five D4Y2-Ss being engaged in combat. The unit's most successful pilot was PO Yoshimitsu Naka, who flew with navigator Ens Hisao Kanazawa. Naka originally saw combat in E13A1 'Jake' two-seat floatplanes with 936th Kokutai from Labuan, off the northwest coast of Borneo, claiming a US dive-bomber damaged and two torpedo-boats sunk at night during the course of 56 sorties between 15 April and 30 September 1943. Converting to fighters in 1944, he was posted to 302nd Kokutai and flew the Suisei in combat from early 1945.

Participating in the defence of the Kanto Plain, north of Tokyo, Naka chased down a B-29 on 20 February as it commenced its return flight after attacking the capital. Making a series of 'dive-and-zoom' attacks, he succeeded in shooting the bomber down. This was the first victory credited to 2nd Hikotai. Naka would repeat this success a further four times (including on the nights of 13 April and 24 May), claiming a quartet of B-29s destroyed using the same tactics. By June, the aircraft flown by Naka and Kanazawa wore nine B-29 victory markings for five confirmed and four probable successes. Some of these had come after 302nd Kokutai had sent 12 Gekkos and eight Suisei to Itami to help with the defence of the Hanshin area in western Japan.

This New Year commemorative group photograph of personnel from 302nd Kokutai's 2nd Hikotai Suisei Nightfighter Unit was taken at Atsugi on 2 January 1945 (Tony Holmes Collection)

PO Yoshimitsu Naka (right) was the leading Suisei nightfighter ace, and he is seen here with Lt(jg) Kuramoto. Behind them is the tail of Naka's 'YoD-228', complete with its pilot's victory tally. This aircraft was written off in crash landing on 13 August 1945. Naka survived the war, but Kuramoto was killed in action on 10 June 1945 while attempting to intercept a B-29 raid on Tokyo (Tony Holmes Collection)

APPENDICES

COLOUR PLATES

1
D4Y2 'Ko-DY-29' of Naval Air Technical Arsenal, Yokosuka, Japan, 1943

Despite experiencing early flight-testing success, simulated dive-bombing with the D4Y1 under full weapons load revealed that the aircraft was susceptible to wing flutter problems that could lead to potentially catastrophic structural failure. The D4Y2 depicted here performed successful service trials in 1943 after the flutter problems had been eradicated. It is believed that 'Ko-DY-29' also subsequently became the first Suisei to be fitted with the more powerful Atsuta Model 32 engine, thus creating the D4Y2 Model 12 (the first production example of which was completed on 15 May 1944). The distinguishing external feature of the D4Y2 Model 12 from the D4Y1 Model 11 was a very small bulge on the upper line of the cowling just in front of the gun/bombsight immediately ahead of the windscreen. Extant photographs of this aircraft, however, do not show this, either because it was the first trial installation or, more likely, the images were taken before the new engine had been installed.

2
D4Y1 '01-065' of 501st Kokutai, Truk Atoll, Central Pacific, early 1944

Equipped with 20 strengthened D4Y1s, 501st Kokutai gave the Suisei its operational debut as a dive-bomber from Rabaul in October 1943. The aircraft would also play a minor part in ill-fated Operation *Ro-Go* the following month. 501st Kokutai was transferred to Truk in late January when Rabaul was all but abandoned by the IJNAF. It was wiped out at Truk in Operation *Hailstone* in February 1944.

3
D4Y1 '01-070' of 501st Kokutai, Rabaul, New Britain, December 1943

'01-070' was captured pretty much intact by the 1st Marine Division at Hoskins airfield, on the north coast of New Britain, in early May 1944, the aircraft having been operational with 501st Kokutai while that unit was based at Rabaul. Based on documentation in 501st Kokutai's combat log, this aircraft probably came to grief at this airfield on 28 January 1944.

4
D4Y1 '07-315' of 503rd Kokutai, Kisarazu, Japan, March 1944

This D4Y1 was one of 36 Suisei assigned to 503rd Kokutai, the aircraft being allocated to the air group's 107th Hikotai. The unit was deployed to Truk Atoll on 10 March 1944 and took part in its defence. Following the battle for Truk, the surviving remnants of 503rd Kokutai were deployed to Yap, Wasile and Sorong. Flying from the latter two locations, aircraft mounted ineffectual attacks on Allied warships of TG 77.2 during the Battle of Biak, in Western New Guinea, through to the air group's disbandment on 10 July 1944.

5
D4Y1-C 'Yo-25' of Yokosuka Kokutai, Yokosuka, Japan, April 1944

This reconnaissance Suisei was one of 24 in service with Yokosuka Kokutai in April 1944. The air group also had 36 D4Y1 dive-bombers on strength at this time too, Yokosuka Kokutai performing testing roles during this period. Indeed, the air group had been a service test unit for much of its long history, and it had not fielded frontline hikotai until 1944. Yokosuka Kokutai subsequently committed aircraft to the First Battle of the Philippine Sea and the defence of the Home Islands.

6
D4Y1-C 'Kiji-10' of 121st Kokutai, Tinian, Northern Mariana Islands, May 1944

This D4Y1-C was one of 16 assigned to 121st Kokutai, christened 'Kiji Butai' (Pheasant Corps), and based on Tinian in May 1944. The air group had been formed at Katori on 1 October 1943 and issued with 12 reconnaissance-optimised Suisei and an undisclosed number of Saiun. Its strength had doubled by January 1944, which increased to 48 the following month – just prior to 121st Kokutai being deployed operationally to Tinian, Peleliu and Sorong (in Dutch New Guinea). The air group initially saw action on 20 March when 11 US Navy carriers from TG 58.2 attacked targets on and around Palau in Operation *Desecrate 1*. This particular aircraft participated in search missions for TF 58 during the First Battle of the Philippine Sea on 19 June 1944, when 121st Kokutai suffered horrendous losses to US carrier-based fighters. The air group was disbanded as a result on 10 July 1944.

7
D4Y1 'Taka-3' of 523rd Kokutai, Tinian, Northern Mariana Islands, May 1944

523rd Kokutai split 40+ D4Y1s between airfields on Tinian, Peleliu and Saipan, from where they were heavily committed in the days immediately preceding Operation *A-Go*. The Kokutai lost a number of its aircraft with the capture of Aslito Field, on Saipan, by the US Army's 27th Infantry Division on 18 June, and its remaining aircraft were destroyed during *A-Go* itself. 523rd Kokutai was disbanded on 10 July.

8
D4Y1 'Taka-68' of 523rd Kokutai, Tinian, Northern Mariana Islands, May 1944

This D4Y1 participated in the attack on TF 58 off Saipan during the First Battle of the Philippine Sea, and it was most likely one of the 70+ Suisei shot down during the 'Great Marianas Turkey Shoot' of 19 June 1944. Shorn of its aircraft and crews, the air group was disbanded three weeks later.

9
D4Y1 'Taka-2' of 523rd Kokutai, Tinian, Northern Mariana Islands, June 1944

Like all D4Y1s assigned to 523rd Kokutai in the Northern Mariana Islands in mid-1944, this aircraft has the Japanese kanji character symbolising the 'falcon' as part of its tail code – the air group was also known as the 'Falcon Corps'. This Suisei was captured relatively intact by the US Marine Corps at Ushi Point airfield on 26 July 1944 and later evaluated by Technical Air Intelligence Unit-Pacific Ocean Area.

10
D4Y1-C 'YoD-12' of 302nd Kokutai, Atsugi, Japan, summer 1944

This D4Y1-C was one of a handful of Suisei reconnaissance aircraft assigned to the future nightfighter unit of 302nd Kokutai, which had been established at Kisarazu on 1 March 1944 and transferred to Atsugi later that same month. The air group was initially intended to have been equipped with 48 day fighters and 24 nightfighters, although its 3rd Hikotai was supplied with D4Y1-Cs whilst dive-bomber Suisei were modified into D4Y2-Ss by 2nd Naval Aeronautical Arsenal's Iwakuni Depot.

11
D4Y1 '634-47' of 634th Kokutai, Kure, Japan, September 1944

This D4Y2 was part of a mixed air group that was to be deployed on board the hybrid carriers *Ise* and *Hyuga*, but which ultimately served as a land-based unit. Participating in the defence of Formosa and in the Second Battle of the Philippines, 634th Kokutai's modest force of D4Y1s (and more numerous A6M5 fighters) was expended in combat and the air group was eventually reformed with reconnaissance floatplanes.

12
D4Y2 '653-292' of 653rd Kokutai, Iwakuni, Japan, October 1944

This D4Y2 was one of just nine Suisei assigned to 653rd Kokutai and based at Iwakuni in October 1944. This unit had been established there following the amalgamation of the air groups assigned to the carriers *Chitose*, *Chiyoda* and *Zuiho* on 15 February 1944. Initially, 653rd Kokutai possessed no Suisei, but in September 263rd Hikotai joined the air group, bringing with it 48 aircraft – three of which were D4Ys. The total number of Suisei had grown to nine by 1 October, but they were not embarked in the carriers (*Chitose*, *Chiyoda* and *Zuiho*) assigned to 3rd Koku Sentai due to the vessels' shortened flightdecks.

13
D4Y2 '01-055' of 701st Kokutai, Clark Field, the Philippines, October 1944

Initially issued with D3A 'Vals' when formed in February 1944, 701st Kokutai slowly switched to brand new D4Y2s from October – on the 1st of that month 102nd Hikotai had eight Suisei and 103rd Hikotai had ten. Deploying to Clark Field on 21 October, the Kokutai remained in-theatre through to 15 November, when it was withdrawn to Kokubu to re-equip.

14
D4Y3 '50' of 5th Attack Hikotai (possibly assigned to 634th Kokutai), Clark Field, the Philippines, late 1944

The exact significance of the two-digit markings seen on this aircraft, and a number of other D4Y3s captured by American troops when Clark Field was overrun in February 1945, has not been definitively identified to date. It is believed, however, that they do not represent a specific operational unit per se, but rather a marking applied at the Aichi factory to newly completed aircraft – '50' are the last two digits of the manufacturer's construction number (3950) for this Suisei. The aircraft were assigned to 5th Hikotai as attrition replacements, and they had been captured before the delivery number could be changed. 5th Hikotai was involved in a general all-out attack on US forces fighting in the city of Tacloban, on Leyte, on 27 November 1944.

15
D4Y3 '57' of 5th Attack Hikotai (possibly assigned to 634th Kokutai), Clark Field, the Philippines, late 1944

Another late-build Suisei of 634th Kokutai captured intact at Clark Field in February 1945, this aircraft (construction number 3957) was deemed to be the most intact example of a D4Y found on Luzon. Stripped to bare metal and marked with US insignia and the TAIU-SWPA's signature striped rudder, the aircraft was restored to airworthy status over a period of several months and then flight-tested in the Philippines before eventually being scrapped there.

16
D4Y3 '73' of 5th Attack Hikotai (possibly assigned to 634th Kokutai), Clark Field, the Philippines, late 1944

This aircraft (construction number 3973) was also a late-build Suisei of 634th Kokutai captured intact at Clark Field in February 1945. All three D4Y3s depicted in profile artwork were almost certainly assigned to 5th Hikotai.

17
D4Y3 '01-262' of 1001st Kokutai, Hiro, Japan, early 1945

1001st Kokutai was responsible for the transportation of replacement aircraft and parts to kokutai serving overseas. Christened the 'Wild Goose Corps', it flew Suisei to units in Formosa and the Philippines.

18
D4Y3 '252-54' of 252nd Kokutai, Katori, Japan, March 1945

Assigned to 5th Hikotai, this D4Y3 of 252nd Kokutai was photographed at Katori airfield on 30 March 1945 as FPO1c Yoshiji Takeda and FPO2c Shigeki Yamaguchi prepared to depart in it for Kokubu airfield to participate in the defence of Okinawa. Above the aircraft number is a painted rendition of the 'Z' Flag, symbolising the IJN's victory over the Russian fleet at the Battle of Tsushima in May 1905. This flag, when flown alone on the mast of a Japanese warship, meant 'The fate of the Empire rests on the outcome of this battle'. This aircraft failed to reach Kokubu on the 31st, its crew being killed when they crashed near Kanbara, in Shizuoka Prefecture, after flying into a weather front. A second D4Y3 and its crew were also lost, with a further three Suisei being destroyed in crash landings.

19
D4Y3 '721-207' of 721st Kokutai, Kanoya, Japan, March 1945

This air group was intended from the first as a unit to operate MXY7 Ohka piloted rocket bombs, with G4M2E 'Betty' bombers as motherships. A few D4Y3s were also assigned to 721st Kokutai, as the original intention was to coordinate Ohka operations with those of Suisei dive-bombers. To that end, D4Ys flew a few training missions with 'Betty'/Ohka formations from Kanoya, but the combination was never tried operationally.

20
D4Y2 '131-62' of 131st Kokutai, Kanoya, Japan, April 1945

This dive-bomber served as part of the 'Hibiscus Corps', as 131st Kokutai became known following its posting to Kanoya from Katori in April 1945. Established at Yokosuka in July 1944, the air group had initially comprised hikotai equipped with D4Y1-C reconnaissance aircraft and J1N1-S nightfighters. 131st Kokutai switched exclusively to D4Y2s in December when it received 48 dive-bombers, only to then be issued with A6M5 'nightfighters' in April 1945. The 131st flew both 'Zekes' and Suisei through to war's end, undertaking night attack missions against enemy airfields on Okinawa and targeting Allied ships sailing in the Ryukyus – its first such attack sortie, involving four 'Zeke' nightfighters and eight 'Judy' dive-bombers, had taken place on 4 April.

21
D4Y2 '131-49' of 131st Kokutai, Kanoya, Japan, April 1945
This D4Y2 was one of 48 dive-bombers assigned to 131st Kokutai at Kanoya in April 1945, the air group having been equipped with the final Atsuta 32-engined Suisei from December 1944. Just 326 D4Y2s were built by Aichi between April and August 1944.

22
D4Y3 'Yo-207' of Yokosuka Kokutai, Yokosuka, Japan, April 1945
This aircraft from Yokosuka Kokutai has a white Home Defence panel behind the fuselage Hinomaru. It is also marked with Yokosuka Kokutai's distinctive code letter and yellow tail tip stripes.

23
D4Y4 '252-28' of 252nd Kokutai, Katori, Japan, April 1945
This aircraft was one of a number of single-seat Special Attack Suisei assigned to 252nd Kokutai's 3rd Hikotai for use in the defence of Okinawa during April 1945. In the fiercely fought campaign, 3rd Hikotai operated a basic tactical formation of one kutai made up of four aircraft. The lead Suisei would be a two-seat D4Y3, while the other three would be single-seat D4Y4s.

24
D4Y3 '701-122' of 701st Kokutai, Kokubu, Japan, April 1945
Following its near-annihilation in the Philippines in October–November 1944, 701st Kokutai was built back up to strength at Kokubu, on Kyushu, in preparation for the defence of Okinawa. D4Y3s delivered to the air group were split between 103rd, 105th and 251st Hikotais, flying from Kokubu Nos. 1 and 2 airfields. Suisei from 701st Kokutai inflicted significant damage on carriers and destroyers from TF 58 off Kyushu on 18–19 March 1945.

25
D4Y2 'Yo-201' of Yokosuka Kokutai, Yokosuka, Japan, 1945
This dive-bomber belonged to Yokosuka Kokutai's 2nd Hikotai, as indicated by the twin yellow stripes atop the vertical stabiliser. The aircraft served with the air group during the ill-fated defence of the Home Islands, Yokosuka Kokutai also having eight D4Y1-Cs on charge during this late war period.

26
D4Y2-S 'YoD-228' of 302nd Kokutai, Atsugi, Japan, June 1945
This D4Y2-S nightfighter was flown by PO Yoshimitsu Naka and navigator Lt Hisao Kanazawa of 302nd Kokutai from Atsugi in early June 1945, the aircraft being marked with five 'Yae-zakura' (double-petalled cherry blossoms) indicating definite 'shoot downs' and four single-petalled cherry blossoms denoting bombers damaged. Assigned to 302nd Kokutai's 2nd Hikotai, Naka and Kanazawa

would claim their successes – all B-29s – between 20 February and early June 1945 during the IJNAF defence of the Kanto Plain and Hanshin. The 'YoD' portion of this aircraft's tail code indicates that 302nd Kokutai was the fourth air unit directly assigned to Yokosuka Naval District.

27
D4Y1 'Yo-257' of Yokosuka Kokutai, Yokosuka, Japan, summer 1945
This aircraft from Yokosuka Kokutai was eventually fitted with an experimental turbo-supercharger and photographed after war's end parked at Yokosuka airfield surrounded by other IJNAF types flown by the air group.

28
D4Y3 'Ri-266' of Hyakurigahara Kokutai, Kokubu, Japan, August 1945
Major training units stationed in Japan all fielded tokko flights for the Okinawa campaign, with Hyakurigahara Kokutai establishing 2nd Seito-tai at Kokubu's No. 2 airfield in April 1945. By 3 August the air group consisted of 96 carrier fighters, 48 dive-bombers and 60 carrier attack aircraft. The primary dive-bomber fighting force was comprised of D4Y3s, these aircraft featuring the Katakana symbol for 'Ri' (for HyakuRIgahara) on their tails.

29
D4Y3 '601-46' of 601st Kokutai, Koromo, Japan, August 1945
This aircraft is famous for the 'bomb piercing carrier' marking painted on its fuselage just forward of the Hinomaru. What appears to be a horizontal stripe beneath the marking is not paint, but a discolouration effect caused by an access panel for battery replacement having been taped over. 601st Kokutai was originally formed as the air group for the carriers of 1st Koku Sentai. After Operations *A-Go* and *Sho-1*, however, it was reorganised as a land-based formation and was actively deployed during the Okinawa campaign. Its dive-bomber squadron became 1st Attack Hikotai on 20 February 1945, and provided personnel for Special Attack unit 2nd Mitate-tai. By war's end 601st Kokutai had grown into a huge formation, with 100 aircraft on strength.

30
D4Y4 'Ko-DY-42' of Dai-ichi Air Arsenal, Yokosuka, Japan, August 1945
The single-seat D4Y4 was a D4Y3 optimised for kamikaze missions, having had the rear gunner's canopy faired over. It was also RATOG-capable (as seen here), the rockets being used either to allow the Suisei to take off from a small airstrip or to boost its speed when in the final stages of a suicide dive on a ship. Capable of carrying a single 800 kg bomb semi-recessed in the now-doorless bomb-bay, the D4Y4 had a production run of 296 airframes between February and August 1945. This particular aircraft, formerly assigned to Naval Air Technical Arsenal and still carrying that organisation's tail markings, was possibly transferred to Yokosuka Kokutai near war's end for test and evaluation. It had an experimental squared-off top to its fin and rudder.

INDEX

Page numbers in **bold** refer to illustrations some of which have caption locators in brackets.

Abe, Lt Zenji 23–25, 27–29, **27**, 30–31, 43–47
Aichi D3A 6, 8, 9
ailerons 10
Albacore, USS 47
armour protection 7, 12, 13, 15, 29

Belleau Wood, USS 47
bombs
    1764-lb No. 80 Mk 5 Land Bomb 83
    No. 25 Model 1 Bomb 68
    No. 25 Ordinary Bomb **31**
    phosphorous bombs 21–22
    Type 2 No. 50 Model 1 Ordinary Bomb 68, 71, **71**, 75
Bunker Hill, USS 31, 43, 44, 45, **45**, 69

Cabot, USS 25, 44, 69, 70
catapult equipment 12, 13
Cavalla, USS 47
Chichi Jima 29, 75, 76
Chitose (ship) 27, 53, 54
Chiyoda (ship) 27, 53, 54
Coleman, Lt Thaddeus 82
Coral Sea, USS 30
cowlings 14, **14**
Curtiss SB2C Helldiver 15

D4Y "Judy"
    carrier landings 27
    kamikaze tactics 66–68
    markings **37, 42, 48**, 94, 95
    reporting name 6, 12
defence plans, *Sho-1, Sho-2*, and *Sho-3*: 49, 51, 53
design and development 7, 8–15
dive bombing raids 43, 44–47, **45**, 51, 52–53, **52**, 54, 57–58, 61
dogfights 31–32, 57

engines 10–11, **10**, 12, 13–14, **13**, 15, **22, 23**, 24
Enterprise, USS 16, 77, 84, **85**
Essex USS 31, 32, 70–71, **70, 71**, 74, 81

Formosa 49–58, 74
Franklin, USS 6, 77–78, **78**
fuel tanks 9, 12, 17–18, 29, **29**

Grumman fighter planes (Hellcats) 45–46, 47, 58
Guam 30, 43–44
gun/bomb sights **26, 50, 64**

Halsey, Adm. William F. 20, 50
Halsey Powell, USS 78–79
Hancock, USS 52, 69, 78, 79, 83–84
Hayde, Lt(jg) Frank 26
Haynsworth, USS 82
Heinkel He118 V4 (DXHe1) 8, **9**
Hirohito, Emperor 87, 88
Hiryu (ship) 18, **18**
Hiyo (ship) 23, 24, 43, 48
Home Islands 86–88, **86, 87, 88**
Hornet, USS 16, 48

Iguchi, Lt Yonosuke 55, 56, 57, 58, 72
Iida, Lt Fusata 60
Illustrious, HMS 82–83
Imperial Japanese Naval Air Force (IJNAF) 6, 7, 8, 9, 10, 15, 26–27, 48, 52, 60, 61, 80, 86
    151st Kokutai 19, **19**, 20, 22
    153rd Kokutai 51
    210th Kokutai **61**
    253rd Kokutai 19
    302nd Kokutai **90**, 91, **92**
    501st Kokutai 20, 21, **21**, 22, 25, **33**
    503rd Kokutai 23, **24**, 26, **26, 31, 34**, 93
    523rd Kokutai **22**, 23, 30, **30, 35, 48**
    601st Kokutai 23, 28, 74–75, **75, 86**
    652nd Kokutai 23–25, 27

653rd Kokutai **49, 52**, 53
701st Kokutai **54**, 58, 88
Tokubetsu Kogeki units 61
Imperial Japanese Navy (IJN) 60–61
    1st Koku Sentai 21, 22, 23, 28, 31, 43, 47–48
    2nd Koku Sentai 43
    3rd Koku Sentai 31
    11th Koku Kantai 20
    Combined Fleet 16, 17, 20, 26–27
    Kido Butai (Mobile Force) 16, 17
    Occupation Force 17
Independence, USS 69
instrument panels **14**
Intrepid, USS 69, 70
Iwo Jima 29, 48, 62, 74–75

Junyo (ship) 23, 24, 27, 28, 43, 44

Kaigun Koku Gijutsusho 9, 10, 12, 15, 17
kamikaze missions 7, 59–88, **59**
    attack-run tactics 65–66
    avoiding interception 63
    collision points 66
    D4Y "Judy" tactics 66–68
    death in battle ethos 59
    first recorded attack 69, **69**
    flight profiles 67–68
    Home Islands 86–88, **86, 87, 88**
    jibaku acts 59–60
    number of attacks and success rates 66
    Okinawa 79–85, **80, 81, 82, 84, 85**
    operations in the Philippines 69–73, **69, 70, 71**
    radar detection avoidance 64, 67
    tactics and techniques, evolution of 62–66
    US Navy report on 62–66
    visual detection avoidance 64–65
Kamikaze Tokubestsu Kofekitai 54
Kawasaki Ki-61 'Tony' 20, 21, 22, 26, 29, 30, 71–72
Keokuk, USS 75–76
Kitkun Bay, USS 69, **69, 70**
Koga, Adm. Mineichi 20
Komatsu, WO Sakio 47
Kozono, Lt Cdr Yasuna 89–90, 91
Kurotori, Lt Shiro 91
Kyushu 76–77

Lamson, USS 71–72
Langley, USS 74, 79
Lexington, USS 31
Leyte Gulf, Battle of 52, 53, 61, 69
Lippmann, David H. 77–78
losses 12, 13, 21, 22, 29, 31, 43, 48, 60
    United States Navy 60, 66, 69, 71, 78, 83
Louisville, USS 73

MacArthur, Gen. Douglas 49, 50
McCampbell, Cdr David 31–32
machine guns 11, 13, 14
maintenance **22, 23, 24**
Mariana Islands 23, 27, 28, 29, 49–50
Midway, Battle of 6, 16–18, 60
Mindoro Island 72–73
Miyauchi, Lt Yasunori 43
Monterey, USS 44

Nagumo, V. Adm. Chuichi 16, **17**
Naka, PO Yoshimitsu 92, **92**
Nakajima C6N1 'Myrt' 14
Nakajima Ens Yonekichi 25, 43, 44, 45, 46, 47
navigation skills 29
Navy Carrier Reconnaissance Plane Saiun ('Painted Cloud') Model 11: 14–15
Nay Experimental 13-Shi Carrier Borne Bomber 6, **6**, 8–11, 17–18
New Operational Policy 20
Nimitz, Adm. Chester W. 49, 50
Nooy, Lt(jg) Cornelius 25–26

Obuchi, Lt Keizo 17
Okinawa 62, 67, 68, 76

kamikaze missions 79–85, **80, 81, 82, 84, 85**
Onishi, V. Adm. Takijiro 61, 69
Operation *A-Go* 23, 27, 28–29
Operation *Desecrate 1* 25
Operation *Hailstone* 22, 25
Operation *Love III* 72
Operation *MI* 16
Operation *Ro-Go* 20
"out-of-range" tactics 28–29, 47
oxygen starvation 44
Ozawa, V.Adm. Jisaburo 28, 30–31, 47–48, 53–54, **53**

P-38 Lightning 21, 56, 57, 58
Philippine Sea, First Battle of the 23, 29, 51, 60–61
Philippines 48, 49–58
    kamikaze missions 69–73
Princeton, USS 6, 52–53, **52**

Rabaul 19, 20–22, 50
radar 64, 67
range capabilities 9, 12, 28–29
RATOG (rocket-assisted take-off gear) 14, 15, **15**, **42, 82**, 95
reconnaissance 12, 17, 18, 19, 25, **29**, 51, 54, 72
Roosevelt, Franklin D. 50
Rota airfield 46–47, **46**
Royal Navy 85, 86
Ryuho (ship) 23, 43

Saipan 30, 43–44
San Jacinto, USS 29–30
Santa Cruz, Battle of 18, 19, 60
Saratoga, USS 75
Shokaku (ship) 18, 19, 20, 23, 28, 47
Soryu (ship) **16**, 17, 18
South Dakota, USS 31
speed 9, 11, 12, 24, 25
St Lo, USS 69, **69**
submarines 28, 47
Suzuki, Lt Fumio **84**

Taiho (ship) 23, 28, 31, 47
Takaomi, Lt **87**
Takeda, FPO1c Yoshiji **80, 81**
Ten-Go Operation Plan 79–80
Ticonderoga, USS **70**, 71, **71**, 74
training 25, 67
trials and tests 11, 14, 17–18
Truk 20, 22, 25, 26, 50
Type 99 (D3A1) 24, 25

Ugaki, V. Adm. Matome 7, 79, 88, **88**
United States Navy 28, 49–50
    Third Fleet 50, 53
    Fifth Fleet 28
    Pacific Fleet 16, 20
    Fast Carrier Task Force 51
    Task Force (TF) 38: 22, 50, 51, 86
    Task Force (TF) 58: 22, 30, 76–77, 80
    TG 38.2: 69, 70
    TG 38.3: 70, 74
    TG 58.2: 25, 26, 43, 44, 48
    losses 60, 66, 69, 71, 78, 83
    report on kamikaze tactics 62–66
USAAF Fifth Air Force 21

Wasp, USS 31, 43, 44, 45, 78
Wenger, Michael 47, 23, 43, 45
wings 10, 11, 12

Yamaguchi, FPO2c Shigeki **80, 81**
Yamakawa, WO Shinsaku 54–58
Yamamoto, Adm. Isoroku 16, 17
Yamana, Masao 9
Yamato (ship) 83, 84
Yorktown, USS 16, 18, 79

"Z" flags 31
Zuiho (ship) 20, 23, 27, 53, 54
Zuikaku (ship) 20, 28, 47, 53, 54